Ivor Powell

Honey From The Rock

Spiritual Refreshment from the Rock of Ages

kregel
PUBLICATIONS

Grand Rapids, MI 49501

*Honey from the Rock: Spiritual Refreshment
from the Rock of Ages*

Copyright © 1996 by Ivor Powell

Published in 1996 by Kregel Publications, a division of
Kregel, Inc., P.O. Box 2607, Grand Rapids, MI 49501.
Kregel Publications provides trusted, biblical publications
for Christian growth and service. Your comments and suggestions are valued.

Cover Photograph: Patricia Sgrignoli, POSITIVE IMAGES
Cover Design: Alan G. Hartman

Library of Congress Cataloging-in-Publication Data
Powell, Ivor, 1910–
    Honey from the rock: spiritual refreshment from the
rock of ages / Ivor Powell.
        p.   cm.
    Includes index.
    1. Bible—Meditations. 2. Bible—Devotional use.
I. Title.
BS483.5.P68   1996   220.6—dc20   96-10318
                                                 CIP

ISBN 0-8254-3547-1

Printed in the United States of America
1 2 3 4 5 / 00 99 98 97 96

CONTENTS

PREFACE

When Moses delivered his final speech to the children of Israel, he reminded them of the continuing faithfulness of God. Remembering the experiences in the wilderness, he said: "He made you to suck honey from the rock" (Deut. 32:13). Much later the Lord used Asaph, a musician in the tabernacle, to chide the nation. He said if they had obeyed the commandments they would have been given "honey out of the rock" (Ps. 81:16). One wonders if somewhere in Hebrew history such an event had taken place; that a bee's nest had been discovered amidst rocky terrain, and these suggestive Scriptures were based on that discovery. Moses explained that God was the Rock (see Deut. 32:4). The Lord has always been the source of spiritual nourishment and satisfaction. Innumerable people of successive generations have proved this to be true.

I am indebted to the patriarch and Asaph for supplying the title for this book. I have found honey in the Rock of Ages, and these Bible studies are sent forth with the prayer that many pastors will find in them food for the soul and inspiration for sermons.

Once again I express my gratitude to Kregel Publications of Grand Rapids, Michigan. They are great friends whose excellence in the world of books speaks eloquently. They will be entrusted with this volume, and will produce something exceptionally attractive. I also thank my wife, Betty, whose patient and skillful editing made this book possible. Her scrutiny has polished what I hope will prove to be a diamond of exceptional beauty.

IVOR POWELL

SECTION ONE
The Old Testament

THE DANGER OF BEING TOO LATE

*Today if ye will hear his voice, harden not your hearts
(Heb. 3:7–8).*

My spirit shall not always strive with man (Gen. 6:3).

Some years ago in one of the rescue missions in the state of
New York, a prominent attorney told how he had become a
Christian. He described how, at the age of twenty-four, he
married a very talented and beautiful young woman, but unfortunately at that time, he had been almost an atheist and
persisted in trying to destroy his wife's faith. After a few
years a baby arrived, and the adoring mother took her daughter to the church services. The years passed, and the girl became a charming young lady who leaned increasingly toward
her father's way of life. She ceased attending church, and he
arranged special outings to provide excuses for his daughter's
actions.

When she was twenty, she was engaged to be married and
later went with friends on a boating vacation in Pennsylvania.
One foolish young man began rocking the boat, and it eventually
capsized, throwing its occupants into the icy water. They were
all excellent swimmers, but unwisely, instead of drying their
clothing, they drove home in wet garments. The girl contracted
pneumonia and became gravely ill. When she realized death
was approaching, she sobbed and said, "Daddy, I don't want to
die." The attorney paused, for it was difficult to control his
emotion. The girl's voice was getting weaker when she said,
"Daddy, you have been saying all along there was no need to
worry about religion, if I did what was right, heaven would
take care of itself. Mother disagreed, telling me that I needed
Christ as my Savior. Daddy, now that I am dying, will you
please tell me which way I should go—Mother's way or yours?"
The father leaned forward and, grasping his daughter, nearly
lifted her from the bed. Holding her tightly to his chest, he
whispered, "Darling, if you have a moment to spare, for Christ's
sake, for your own sake, for your mother's sake, and for your

9

hard-hearted daddy's sake, take Mother's way." That sorrowful parent explained that by the time he had lowered the frail body into the bed, she was gone. Then he stepped into the aisle and, pulling desperately at his gray hair, said, "Brothers and sisters, only God knows whether my darling had enough time to take her mother's way."

This disturbing story illustrates the three facts found in the introductory verse. (1) *"TODAY"—A Priceless Opportunity.* Yesterday has gone forever. Tomorrow may never arrive. Today is a part of time which is fleeting. If something needs to be done urgently, wisdom whispers, *"DO IT."* (2) *IF YE HEAR HIS VOICE"—A Personal Obedience.* When any person is able to hear the voice of God, it is the guarantee the Lord continues to speak. Wisdom suggests, *"LISTEN."* (3) *"HARDEN NOT YOUR HEART"—A Possible Obstinacy.* When the Savior seeks admission to the human heart, only two responses are possible. Do nothing and let Him remain outside, or open the door to make His entrance possible. Wisdom urges, *"ACT."*

History teaches that occasionally opportunity comes only once. What is done then may decide destiny. A lost chance may never return. God, through Isaiah, said: "Come *NOW*, and let us reason together, saith the LORD: though your sins be as scarlet, they shall be as white as snow; though they be red like crimson, they shall be as wool" (Isa. 1:18). God says, "COME NOW." People who say "We will come someday" may arrive too late!

The Procrastination of a Multitude

They did eat, they drank, they married wives, they were given in marriage, until the day that Noah entered into the ark, and the flood came, and destroyed them all (Luke 17:27).

And [God] spared not the old world, but saved Noah the eighth person, a preacher of righteousness (2 Peter 2:5).

The apostle Peter described Noah as "A preacher of righteousness." The statement is intriguing. At that time there was no Gospel to be preached, and the Almighty was regarded

10

as the austere, but omnipotent, Ruler of the Universe. He could, and would, punish people who displeased Him. The Ten Commandments had not been given, and therefore Noah was limited in his knowledge. He denounced the conduct of his neighbors, but the situation described by Peter is thought-provoking. "For if God spared not the angels that sinned, but cast them down to hell and delivered them unto chains of darkness to be reserved unto judgment" (2 Peter 2:4). The events that happened during Noah's lifetime were abominable and disgusting. He denounced what he saw and probably became an object of scorn. It was only when the rising waters of the flood shattered the self-confidence of the population, that unbelievers began to realize their danger.

The door of the ark had been closed. Rain was falling from the sky, and the scoffers who had ignored the warning of Noah could not believe what was happening. Water had already covered the ground, and the waves were washing against the strange vessel on which Noah had labored so long. The sky was filled with ominous clouds, and people were becoming alarmed. For many years they had laughed at the strange preacher and considered him to be a foolish old fellow who had stayed in the sunshine too long! The idea of water coming from the sky was ludicrous, for until that time the earth had been watered by dew.

The arrival of many animals only aroused curiosity. When the door of the ark was closed, and another seven uneventful days passed, possibly the observers began speculating how long it would be before Noah, in search of fresh air, opened the door.

And it came to pass after seven days, that the waters of the flood were upon the earth . . . all the fountains of the great deep broken up, and the windows of heaven were opened. And the rain was upon the earth forty days and forty nights (Gen. 7:10–12).

Frightened people began climbing to higher ground, and others tried to cling to the ship, which was already riding gracefully upon the rising water. Unfortunately, they had waited too long to respond to the invitation of Jehovah. It is thought-provoking that Jesus said, "But as the days of Noah were, so shall also the coming of the Son of man be" (Matt. 24:3, 7).

The Procrastination of a Mob

During my stay in Australia I was entertained in the home of Mr. Walter Beasly, a prosperous business executive in the city of Melbourne. He was a very keen Christian who helped to finance several archaeological expeditions in the Middle East. He supplied the following details.

When he spoke of the destruction of Sodom and Gomorrah, he explained that certain discoveries had enabled the scientists, in thought at least, to reconstruct the ancient tragedy. (1) They discovered beneath the ancient site evidence of a burnt-out oil field. (2) On either side of the district was a vertical fault in the strata of the earth. (3) Deep in the ground were immense deposits of rock salt, but in the immediate area of Sodom the salt was on the surface. Evidently it was carried out of its original habitat by up-rushing oil which was flung into the air to drop as a gigantic snow storm. Apparently a tremendous earthquake shook the area; the earth slipped between the faults, and the pressure on the oil field forced enormous quantities of oil to the surface. When this became ignited, Sodom and Gomorrah were destroyed by falling masses of flame. Lot's wife was instructed to flee for her life, but she disobeyed. When the woman turned to gaze at her former home, the earth split around her and she was trapped. She was quickly covered by the salt and died of suffocation.

Against that background it is possible to understand the ancient story. Sodom was inhabited by homosexuals who refused to abandon their evil practices. Their doom became inevitable. Paul described a similar situation when he wrote to the Christians in Rome.

Wherefore **God also gave them up** to uncleanness through the lusts of their own hearts, to dishonour their own bodies

12

between themselves . . . **For this cause God gave them up** unto vile affections: for even their women did change the natural use into that which is against nature: And likewise also the men, leaving the natural use of the woman, burned in their lust one toward another, men with men working that which is unseemly, and receiving in themselves that recompense of their error which was meet. And even as they did not like to retain God in their knowledge, **God gave them over** to a reprobate mind, to do those things which are not convenient (Rom. 1:24–28).

Vast numbers of people are dying of a loathsome disease which apparently is incurable. It has spread through a situation such as existed in the two ancient cities, but is to be regretted that innocent people suffer because of the sins of others. It is evident that when God gives up on any man, that soul is beyond redemption. This is accentuated by the text quoted at the beginning of this study: *"Today*, if ye hear his voice, harden not your heart."

The Procrastination of a Monarch

But when Pharaoh saw that there was respite, he hardened his heart, and harkened not unto them; as the Lord had said (Exod. 8:15).

Pharaoh was thought by his people to be a god; but perhaps in his own estimation, he was even greater. It is always dangerous when a self-made deity worships at his own shrine. The arrogant ruler detested Moses and Aaron who had become a daily annoyance. Nevertheless, he was disturbed, for the Hebrew leaders possessed strange powers. They demanded the liberation of the slaves and warned Pharaoh of retribution. God had informed His servants that the ruler of Egypt would not respond favorably, but it is doubtful whether they believed what they were told. No man could resist Jehovah; Pharaoh would be compelled to yield. Sometimes God's servants may be carried away with their own enthusiasm. The king hardened his heart as the Lord predicted. Terrible plagues devastated the country, but after promising to cooperate, the ruler changed his mind.

It is possible to become so set in one's ways that change becomes impossible. A man may be dead before he dies! Everything might have been different had the king obeyed the voice of God. One fact is easy to understand. Had the ruler been wise, he would have lived longer. When the water of the Red Sea overwhelmed the Egyptian army and Pharaoh died with his men, it was too late to repent. When God says "Come now," only foolish people reply, "I will do it tomorrow." The final act of rebellion led to a premature death, but it is difficult to avoid the conclusion the king deserved his fate. God would inevitably fulfill His plans, but the Egyptians needed to be taught a lesson. Pharaoh did not recognize—as Daniel later said to king Belshazzar "the God in whose hand thy breath is" (see Dan. 5:2–3).

The Procrastination of a Man

> Then Judas, which had betrayed him, when he saw that he was condemned, repented himself, and brought again the thirty pieces of silver to the chief priests and elders, Saying, I have sinned in that I have betrayed the innocent blood. And they said, What is that to us? see thou to that. And he cast down the pieces of silver in the temple, and departed, and went and hanged himself (Matt. 27:3–5).

The pathetic statement: "Judas repented himself" has been used to distort the truth. Cinematography depicts Judas going to Calvary to seek forgiveness from the Savior. Authors in search of happy endings for their stories describe how, in the darkest hour of the betrayer's life, the love of Christ reached out to reclaim the degraded sinner. These people ignore the fact that when the Lord prayed for His disciples He said, "While I was with them in the world, I kept them in thy name: those that thou gavest me, I have kept, and *none of them is lost, but the son of perdition*; that the scripture might be fulfilled" (John 17:12). Judas was a lost soul whom even Christ could not save. He repented, but unfortunately his day

14

of grace had terminated. When immediate action is necessary, delay is dangerous. The Scriptures say: "Behold, *now* is the accepted time; behold, *now* is the day of salvation" (2 Cor. 6:2).

> While the voice of Jesus calls you
> Be in time.
> If in sin you longer wait,
> You may find no open gate;
> And your cry be just too late,
> Be in time.
> William J. Kirkpatrick

And it came to pass after seven days, that the waters of the flood were upon the earth (Gen. 7:10).

John Newton, who lived from 1725 until 1807, was at one time a slave trader transporting victims from Africa to America. Ultimately this notorious sea captain became an ordained minister in the Anglican church. His influence was felt throughout Britain, and although his lifespan was eighty-two years, some of his hymns will last for ever. He spoke incessantly of the grace of God which had miraculously changed his life and, when close to death, exclaimed, "My memory is almost gone, but I remember two things. That I am a great sinner, and that Christ is a great Savior." Engraved on his tombstone in the parish graveyard at Olney, England, is an inscription, which he wrote:

John Newton, once an infidel and Libertine, a servant of slavers in Africa, was by the rich mercy of our Lord and Savior Jesus Christ, preserved, restored, pardoned, and appointed to preach the Faith he had long labored to destroy.

He requested those words be placed on his grave so that the testimony given throughout his ministry might continue. He was one of the greatest evangelical preachers of the eighteenth century, and among the first clergymen to become interested in church hymnals. Among his many compositions was the hymn which has become an international favorite. *Amazing Grace* has won for itself an abiding place in the hearts of innumerable Christians. The first and last verses of this inspired poetry cannot be forgotten.

> Amazing grace! How sweet the sound—
> That saved a wretch like me!
> I once was lost but now am found,
> Was blind but now I see.

When we've been there ten thousand years,
Bright shining as the sun,
We've no less days to sing God's praise
Than when we'd first begun.

God's Grace Extended

After seven days (Gen. 7:10).

Long ago when the world was young, a baby was born who was destined to become famous. He was not of royal lineage, and yet he became better known than kings. His father, Enoch, was a prophet who daily walked with God. When the man saw the child for the first time, God whispered, "You must call him Methuselah." As far as is known, that name has only been used once. Dr. Lang, the noted commentator, says it was prophetical. "It shall not come until he die." Enoch was capable of foretelling the future, and since the great flood came in the year the man died, it is impossible to dispute the accuracy of the prediction.

Methuselah lived for nine hundred and sixty-nine years. His longevity is easily explained. The extent of God's mercy was indicated by the length of the man's life. Noah, for instance, lived 950 years. The longer he lived, the more opportunities Noah had to preach. It was truly amazing that Jehovah extended His period of grace for nearly a thousand years. Nevertheless, the people were too blind to see the significance of what was taking place. There was no reason why the Lord should care for such sinful people, but He did!

Noah never lost an opportunity to warn the people who came to see his ship. The audience must have been large, for the vessel was a great attraction. The strange old preacher evidently had quaint ideas, for he predicted there would be no need to take the ark to the ocean; it would come to him. When animals of all kinds began to arrive, the excitement of the onlookers increased enormously; this was the world's first circus. Calmly, Noah proceeded with the embarkation, and finally, he and his family entered the ark and the door was closed.

The onlookers were probably amused, and if gambling were known at the time, the bookmakers were soon offering odds

17

regarding the reappearance of the foolish old man. How could people exist for days in a polluted atmosphere? They were either mentally deranged or fools! The ship was ready to sail, and every necessity had been foreseen. Probably Noah said to his sons, "Let's go," but the Lord whispered, "Not yet." He waited seven days to give foolish people another week in which to seek admittance into God's ship of destiny.

God's Grace Expanded

And the LORD spake unto Moses, saying, Speak unto the children of Israel, saying, If any man of you or of your posterity shall be unclean by reason of a dead body, or be in a journey afar off, yet he shall keep the passover unto the LORD. The fourteenth day of the second month at even they shall keep it, and eat it with unleavened bread and bitter herbs (Num. 9:9–11).

The eating of the Passover Feast was one of the most solemn occasions in the Hebrew year. Every person was commanded to participate, for this recalled the time when God redeemed Israel from bondage. The commemoration was so important that every parent was responsible for the spiritual education of children. Boys and girls had to be instructed how salvation was made possible through the blood of the lamb. Throughout its long history the nation obeyed that special commandment, and even Jesus joined with others in observing the ancient custom. He gave to it a new meaning by substituting what is now called the Last Supper. The Hebrews honored and revered the Passover more than any other festival, and it has been estimated that during the life of Christ more than three million people attended the feast.

And there were certain men, who were defiled by the dead body of a man, that they could not keep the passover on that day: and they came before Moses and before Aaron on that day. And those men said unto him, We are defiled by the dead body of a man: Wherefore are we kept back, that we may not offer the offering of the LORD in his appointed season among the children of Israel? And Moses said unto them,

Stand still, and I will hear what the LORD will command concerning you (Num. 9:6–8).

Moses was very wise. He had not encountered this problem earlier and had no wish to make a mistake. The questioners were instructed to wait until the problem had been presented before God. It is interesting that for these men Jehovah ordered a second Passover to be arranged thirty days after the first one. This provided an extra opportunity for commercial travelers who journeyed "afar off" and for unclean people to take advantage of God's expanded grace. Defilement of any kind prevented a worshiper from attending the feast, and all graves had to be marked with white signs to warn people about contamination. Every person was obliged to observe this law. That God was willing to arrange another Passover was evidence of His great compassion.

The Hebrews believed they only were recipients of divine blessings. Gentiles were considered to be unclean and undesirable. It was difficult for self-righteous people to believe other nations were also precious in the sight of God. The cleansing of Naaman, the leper, and the acceptance of Ruth, the maiden from Moab, were not favorite stories among the Hebrews. It was even more difficult for Pharisees to believe God could love Gentiles. When the children of Israel heard the first Passover command, they discovered what was in God's mind. When they learned of the second Passover to be held thirty days later, they knew what was in His heart.

God's Grace Exhausted

And the LORD said unto Moses, Rise up early in the morning, and stand before Pharaoh, and say unto him, Thus saith the LORD God of the Hebrews, Let my people go, that they may serve me, For I will at this time send ALL MY PLAGUES upon thine heart, and upon thy servants, and upon thy people, that thou mayest know that there is none like me in all the earth (Exod. 9:13–14).

At the height of their power the Pharaohs of Egypt were

among the greatest military people in existence. Their army was feared by all other nations. No one is sure how the immense pyramids and sphinx were built. During one of my visits to Egypt, I saw the immense preparation being made by the Japanese who thought they could emulate the example of the ancient builders. They planned to erect a new pyramid alongside the old one. They were given permission by the Egyptian government on the condition that if they succeeded, they would dismantle their structure as soon as it was finished. When next I went to Cairo, the equipment had been removed, for the foreigners had abandoned their project. How the original structures were made may remain a secret forever.

During their captivity the children of Israel provided un-limited labor for the taskmasters and perhaps played some part in the erection of those massive monuments.

The Hebrews were slaves for four hundred years and during that time learned how Egyptians worshiped many gods. Each village had its own deity, and pottery unearthed by the archaeologists suggests that animals, stars, and other things were objects of veneration. It was during the latter part of this period that Pharaoh exhausted the patience of God. Moses was told that the Lord would harden the heart of his antagonist (see Exod. 7:3). Later Jehovah allowed the ancient author to understand the true condition of the king who hardened his own heart. Pharaoh was determined to prevent the escape of his captives and opposed every attempt to release them (see Exod. 8:15). The Egyptians worshiped images that could be seen and could not understand how their captives revered One who was invisible.

One wonders why God continued His efforts to change Pharaoh's attitude. The plagues were episodes in a divine attempt to destroy the man's animosity, and Pharoah's destruction proves that frequently even God becomes frustrated and helpless. The Lord's patience with sinful men is very great, but it can end! He says *"COME NOW* and let us reason together" (Isa. 1:18). There may never be a tomorrow. The judgment of God only falls upon people who reject His mercy. No man will be able to say to Him, "If you had only given to me one additional opportunity, I might have "responded."

THE MAN WHO WAS SCARED
AT THE GATE OF HEAVEN

And Jacob awaked out of his sleep, . . . and he was afraid, and
said, How dreadful is this place! this is none other but the
house of God, and this is the gate of heaven (Gen. 28:16–17).

This was true in a dual sense; Jacob slept through the night,
but his soul—until that moment—had never been awake. He
had heard about the God of his ancestors and was probably
acquainted with the brief history of man, but he preferred to
trust himself than in God whom he had never seen. The patriarch was a deceiver who lived by his wits, a schemer who
devised ways to obtain what he desired. Jacob's conduct alien-
ated him from family and friends and made him a fugitive.
Desperately alone, the man had traveled through the desert
and, completely exhausted, hardly knew whether he wanted
to live or die. The water in the goatskin was almost gone. His
body ached, and the sand sticking to his face seemed like
cement. He had reached mountains that were possibly ter-
raced, where rocky peaks stood as sentinels. There was no
vegetation, and gathering rocks, the poor man made a pillow
and, lying upon the ground, fell asleep. His soul was as empty
as the landscape, and at that moment Jacob surely questioned
the conduct which had banished him from society.

As he was enveloped by the stillness of the night, and stars
shone as jewels in a velvet sky, Jacob's mind became a stage
where angels performed in an unfolding drama.

And he dreamed, and behold a ladder set up on the earth, and
the top of it reached to heaven: and behold the angels of God
ascending and descending on it. And behold, the LORD stood
above it (Gen. 28:12).

It was entrancing. The terraces on the hill seemed to have
been transformed into radiant steps reflecting the glory of
God, and the barren landscape had become a scene of

loveliness. Then Jacob stirred uneasily, for above the ladder he saw the Lord.

The Promises of God Were Reliable

When Jehovah had revealed His plans, Jacob must have been astounded, for what he heard was completely unexpected. The Almighty appeared to be overlooking the terrible defects in the fugitive's conduct. He promised to bless and reward the undeserving listener. This was Jacob's first encounter with the Lord, but instead of being elated with the news, the man was filled with fear and said, "How dreadful is this place. This is none other but the house of God, and this is the gate of heaven." It was as though a pauper had been given a priceless treasure only to respond: "This is the worst day of my life." It was evident God was not rewarding any merit in Jacob's life; the man was a cheat and a reprobate. Why then did God treat him favorably? The Lord said:

> And, behold, I am with thee, and will keep thee in all places whither thou goest, and will bring thee again into this land; for I will not leave thee, until I have done that which I have spoken to thee of (Gen. 28:15).

Jacob was receiving his first lesson in righteousness. Jehovah had made a covenant with Abraham, and nothing could change that arrangement (see Gen. 15:18). Neither the scheming of enemies nor the failure of men would be permitted to interfere. He who saw the end from the beginning was capable of removing any obstacle that might arise. God, in response to the Abrahamic covenant, would be the constant guardian of this disappointing runaway. The fact that Jacob responded in such a strange manner revealed how uncomfortable he had become in the presence of the Lord. It is impossible for any man to encounter the glory of God and not feel guilty. Jacob would have appreciated the sentiments expressed by Simon Peter who said to Jesus, "Depart from me; for I am a sinful man, O Lord" (Luke 5:8).

The British statesman, William Ewart Gladstone (1809–

1898), referred to the Bible as "The Impregnable Rock of Holy Scripture." He knew the most reliable foundation upon which a nation or an individual could build was the inspired Word of God. It is a cause for regret that many people have forgotten that profound truth.

The Power of God Was Remarkable

To appreciate the magnitude of God's promise to Jacob, it is necessary to understand the situation that confronted the destitute traveler. He possessed nothing except the clothing he wore. He owned no land, yet God said his seed would possess everything that could be seen in every direction. Jacob was unmarried, but God promised his children would be as numerous as the grains of sand in the desert. Esau, a very angry brother, had vowed to take Jacob's life, but the Lord promised to bring him back safely. Practically penniless, he was to become extremely wealthy. He had no friends, but the Lord would be his constant companion.

These promises reflected the unlimited ability of God to make all things work favorably for the recipient. Yet it did not change the character of the deceiver who continued to be a swindler and a cheat. The way in which later he outwitted his father-in-law, indicated only God can change human nature. It was almost unbelievable that this disappointing man could be made "a prince with God" (see Gen. 32:28).

The reclamation of humanity has always been God's greatest concern. It was easy to bring planets into being but difficult to persuade stubborn sinners to listen to divine reasoning. It is thrilling to know God never abandoned His wayward child. As the master Potter, the Lord remade the marred human vessel into a man of integrity. This was a foreshadowing of other miracles to be seen in the ministry of Jesus of Nazareth.

The Plans of God Were Recommendable

And he called the name of that place Bethel . . . And Jacob vowed a vow, saying, If God will be with me, and will keep me in this way that I go, and will give me bread to eat, and raiment to put on, so that I come again to my father's house in peace;

23

then shall the LORD be my God . . . and of all that thou shalt give me I will surely give a tenth unto thee (Gen. 28:19–22).

Great achievements are never accomplished easily. God created planets in moments, but sometimes it takes a lifetime to bring a prodigal back to his father's home. It is good to know that Jacob never forgot his obligations. He went away distressed but returned, devoted. Throughout the varying experiences, he made many enemies and accumulated great wealth but discovered the best things in life could not be bought. Alas, the man became homesick, and he desired to be united with his family. God was already planning to take him home. Jacob was not troubled about meeting his enraged brother; he believed it was possible to bribe anybody. It was a shock to discover Esau's rage was unabated; he had never forgotten Jacob's treachery, and was determined to be avenged. Becoming afraid, Jacob dispatched his family to a place of safety and "was left alone."

And there wrestled a man with him until the breaking of the day, and when he saw that he prevailed not against him, he touched the hollow of his thigh, and the hollow of Jacob's thigh was out of joint, as he wrestled with him. And he said: Let me go, for the day breaketh. And he [Jacob] said I will not let thee go, except thou bless me. And he [the angel] said unto him, What is thy name? and he said, Jacob. And he said, Thy name shall no more be called Jacob, but Israel: for as a prince hast thou power with God and with men, and hast prevailed. And Jacob asked him, and said, Tell me, I pray thee, thy name. And he said, Wherefore is it that thou dost ask after my name? And he blessed him there. And Jacob called the name of the place Peniel; for I have seen God face to face, and my life is preserved (Gen. 32:24–30).

When at the beginning of his wanderings Jacob saw God he said, "How dreadful is this place; it is the gate of heaven." After he wrestled with the Lord, he believed himself to be the most privileged man in the world. He had traveled from poverty

24

to peace; through darkness to a new day. That experience may still be enjoyed by all who share their lives with God.

The Prediction of God Was Rational

Nathanael answered, and saith unto him, Rabbi, thou art the Son of God; thou art the King of Israel. Jesus answered and said unto him, Because I said unto thee, I saw thee under the fig tree, believest thou? thou shalt see greater things than these. . . . Verily, verily, I say unto you. Hereafter ye shall see heaven open *and the angels of God ascending and descending* upon the Son of man (John 1:49–51).

This reference to Jacob's ladder suggests an important fact. As far as is known, the promise made to Nathanael has never been fulfilled. There were occasions during the ministry of the Lord when angels attended to His need, but none of these related to the promise made by Christ. Angels strengthened Jesus after his temptation (Mark 1:13) and following His ordeal in the Garden of Gethsemane (Luke 22:43). They also announced His resurrection (John 20:12–13), but none of these occasions related to anything seen by Jacob. This suggests the fulfillment of this promise will be seen when the angels rejoice at the coronation of the King of Kings. Christ, the eternal Word, was, still is, and ever will be the channel of communication between God and humanity. Through the Savior we may reach God and the Almighty can reach people. Jacob's ladder appeared in a dream; it soon faded away. Christ is the highway by which the eternal Father will always maintain contact with His children. He remains the glorious reality which can never fade into insignificance.

Then went he [Laban] *out of Leah's tent, and entered into Rachel's tent. Now Rachel had taken the images, and put them in the camel's furniture, and sat upon them. And Laban searched all the tent, but found them not. And she said to her father, Let it not displease my lord that I cannot rise up before thee, for the custom of women is upon me. And he searched, but found not the images (Gen. 31:34–35).*

Rachel was beautiful and desirable. The daughter of a wealthy farmer, she was admired by all the shepherds who watered their sheep at the communal well. Yet she never permitted them to become amorous. She enjoyed their attention but always remained aloof and never became involved in romance. Her father's wealth and reputation were probably a deterrent to overzealous young men. Her sister, Leah, had bewitching eyes but was not as glamorous as the younger girl. Why both remained unmarried remains a mystery, but probably they were protected by their father who thought his daughters too good for the available men.

Then Jacob arrived to ask the whereabouts of his kinsman, Laban. While he was conversing with the shepherds, Rachel arrived with her father's sheep, and he hastily removed the covering from the mouth of the well to help the girl. As she looked at the muscular stranger and appreciated the assistance being given, something stirred within her soul. It was love at first sight.

Rachel escorted Jacob to her home, and an exciting story of intrigue and deception began to unfold. Eventually, after being tricked on his wedding night, Jacob labored until he had earned the right to marry both daughters. As time passed he became wealthy, but the relationship between Laban and Jacob was never amicable; both were swindlers actuated by greed. Then Jacob became homesick and, with the sheepshearing season approaching, began to make plans to leave. He warned his wives to make the necessary preparation, and when Laban went away for three days, Jacob and his family commenced their journey. Rachel stayed a little longer in her home and, seeing her father's idols, stole them.

The Maid and Her Gods... *Defiling*

The theft caused great trouble, for when Laban discovered his idols were missing, he vowed that Jacob would pay with his life. God appeared to the angry man and averted a tragedy which seemed unavoidable. Jacob, who was unaware of Rachel's action, vehemently denied Laban's charges and suggested a search of the entire camp. When his wife saw servants proceeding from tent to tent, she placed the idols in her camel's saddle, sat upon them, and excused herself for remaining seated by saying, "Let it not displease my lord that I cannot rise up before thee, for the custom of women is upon me." Laban accepted her explanation and did not recover his gods. From time immemorial men have debated the reason for Rachel's theft, and various explanations have been given.

Was she scared the idol might assist her father? Some teachers think she feared the gods might inform Laban where to find his runaway daughters. It is difficult to accept this reasoning, for an experienced rancher would know in which direction Jacob had gone. The herd of cattle would leave tracks which could easily be followed.

Did Rachel desire a special keepsake? She was leaving her home and had no guarantee she would see her father again. Did she desire something which would remind her of childhood days, something that would bridge the gulf between her past and future? When she saw the images, on the spur of the moment she stole them.

Was she being mercenary? She hoped all would go well for her husband, but being a cattleman was a precarious occupation. If bad times overtook them, or if enemies stole the cattle, financial resources could be a valuable asset. Idols that were the cherished possession of devotees were often studded with precious stones which, in an emergency, could be sold. Those images could become a means of survival in adversity.

Did she want a backup God? This suggestion is most intriguing. Her family worshiped idols, and as a child she would have participated in the ritual. Her father was a man with two religions. He was aware of Jehovah whom his ancestors had worshiped, but he also liked his idols which never challenged his conduct. It was inspiring to know the God of his fathers could help, but when He did not respond, it was reassuring to have other gods who would be more cooperative. The images were excellent backup deities. Perhaps Rachel acquired these ideas from her father. Did she reason that if her husband's God failed to respond it would be nice to consult her own gods? It may be difficult to decide why she became a thief, but the Scriptures describe other people with similar desires.

The Missionary and His Goal . . . *Defeated*

There is a strange story in the second book of Kings which describes people who tried to walk in two directions at the same time. When the armies of Babylon overran Palestine and many Hebrews were taken as prisoners to a foreign land, the heathen monarch decided to leave behind an army of occupation. He believed this was the best way to prevent an uprising among the Jews who were permitted to stay in their own land. It would also help to colonize the country and extend the empire of Babylon. This appeared to be an excellent plan but, alas, the king ignored Jehovah. When ravenous lions descended from the hills to kill people and devour cattle, the superstitious Babylonians believed the wild beasts were the instruments of Israel's offended God. When they became afraid, they complained to their king. He decided to return one of the captive priests to Samaria to instruct the inhabitants concerning *"the God of the land."*

This unknown missionary traveled from city to city teaching listeners the laws of Moses, and this created a unique situation. The Babylonian immigrants began to fear the Lord but continued to worship idols. They were afraid of Jehovah's lions but, although they gave lip-service to the God of Israel, they continued to revere their own gods. The people appeared to be devout believers but remained idolaters. They were nominal believers who had no love for the Lord.

This was reminiscent of Rachel who had idols in her home. It also describes people whose religion was only a ceremony. When lions of affliction appear, distressed people pray for divine assistance but afterward forget to give thanks, and they return to the gods of their own creation. It is difficult to avoid the conclusion that the ancient priest did his job, but his message was ineffective.

The Murmurers and Their Gospel . . . *Distracting*

Paul's most aggressive opponents were Jews who tried to unite Christianity with Judaism. They professed to be disciples of Christ, but never abandoned the Mosaic law. Their insistence that Gentile men be circumcised led to the first Church Council where Paul said non-Jews should not be compelled to observe laws which were given exclusively to Hebrews. Although James, the president of that august assembly, ruled in favor of Paul, the adversaries did not change their opinion. Throughout the apostle's missionary journeys, they promoted riots which threatened the lives of the preachers.

Many of these obnoxious people claimed to be Christians. They accepted the Messianic claims of Jesus, but believed sinners needed more (the law) upon which to rely. This suggested that if for any reason Christianity failed, they still possessed the teaching of Moses. Here again are found reminders of Rachel who stole her father's gods, and the priest who failed to remove the idols worshiped by his congregation. Paul denounced the teaching of his adversaries and said they should be accursed for preaching another gospel (see Gal. 1:8). The apostle would have appreciated the hymn written by P. B. Bliss:

> Free from the law; O happy condition.
> Jesus hath bled, and there is remission.
> Cursed by the law and bruised by the fall,
> Christ hath redeemed us, Once for all.

Once for all, O Sinner, receive it,
Once for all, O Brother, believe it.
Cling to the Cross, thy burden will fall;
Christ hath redeemed us, Once for all.

The Man and His Guilt . . . *Destroying*

Judas had an incurable disease—the love of money. It spread throughout his being and destroyed his soul. His death was a tragedy, for he had lived with the Great Physician who cured all kinds of sickness. Unfortunately, he thought more of cash than he did of his soul, and ultimately he was buried in a grave for the homeless.

This pathetic man had ambitions to become famous. By night he dreamed of the kingdom of God and by day worked to establish it, hoping to be worthy of a place of eminence when his Leader became the King of Kings. When he met Jesus of Nazareth, he was convinced the Messiah had arrived. It was one of his greatest days when the Lord invited him to become a disciple. He enjoyed fellowship with his new friends and probably worked as hard as any of his colleagues. He became the treasurer of the party, but the inflow of cash was poor, for his Leader never appealed for financial assistance. Occasionally a grateful admirer gave a special offering, but there was never much money in the treasury. This made Judas long fervently for the prosperity which would be commonplace when the Master established His kingdom. Judas hoped he would become the Minister of Finances. One day he took some of the money for his own purposes, and since his books were never audited, no one discovered the theft. Helping himself became standard procedure.

When the bleak winds of adversity began to blow upon the disciples, Judas shuddered. He hoped his Master would succeed, but if He did not, things could be depressing. If Jesus did not take advantage of His popularity, the future could be in jeopardy. He was very apprehensive when the Lord seemed to be unconcerned. Judas sighed. Enthusiasm disappeared from his life. Had he chosen to follow the wrong leader? How could he recoup his losses and make amends for his mistake? His love for money became apparent when he decided to sell his knowledge and cut his losses. Those stingy money-grabbers would pay for information! They might argue and try to swindle him, but whatever he was given would be better than nothing.

Judas was depending upon his business instincts; something could be salvaged for future use. When he had betrayed his Master, his conscience became active, and the precious coins lost their attraction.

> Then Judas, which had betrayed him, when he saw that he was condemned, repented himself, and brought again the thirty pieces of silver to the chief priests and elders, Saying, I have sinned in that I have betrayed the innocent blood. . . . And he cast down the pieces of silver in the temple, and departed, and went and hanged himself (Matt. 27:3–5).

Judas built his house upon sand, and the storms left him homeless! His money could not purchase a dwelling in this world nor the next. He was a man without wisdom.

> I'd rather have Jesus than silver or gold,
> I'd rather be His than have riches untold;
> I'd rather have Jesus than houses or land,
> I'd rather be led by His nail-pierced hand.
>
> That to be the king of a vast domain
> Or be held in sin's dread sway;
> I'd rather have Jesus than anything
> This world affords today.
>
> R. F. Miller

And Deborah, a prophetess, the wife of Lapidoth, she judged Israel at that time. And she dwelt [sat] under the palm tree of Deborah between Ramah and Bethel, in mount Ephraim; and the children of Israel came up to her for judgment (Judg. 4:4–5).

Deborah was the most outstanding lady in Israel's history. During a period when women were only valued as child-bearers, homemakers, and laborers in the fields, she arose from obscurity to become the most important person in the nation. She was a judge, a military general, a ruler, a prophet-ess, a musician, and a poet. She excelled in every quality, and, if for no other reasons, what is known of her life deserves consideration.

This lady was born sometime between the thirteenth and twelfth centuries before Christ, and her parents must have been elated for they gave their child a name which meant honeybee. This suggests they considered her to be small, very active, and the producer of sweetness. Maybe the name was prophetic, for the baby was destined to reach a place of un-precedented excellence. No other details of her childhood are known, but when she became an adult, she was given in mar-riage to a man called Lapidoth of whom nothing else is known. She must have been good, gracious, and wise, for when God appointed judges to rule the land, Deborah was the only wom-an chosen. She held her court beneath a great palm tree that was later named in her honor. This was astonishing for no other woman in Biblical history shared that distinction. The Bible says:

And when the LORD raised them up judges, then the LORD was with the judge, and delivered them [the children of Israel] out of the hand of their enemies all the days of the judge (Judg. 2:18).

Israel's transgressions were great, and in a period when individuals pleased themselves, law and order were ignored.

The nation was dominated by aggressors, the chief of which were the kings of Syria and Canaan. The Promised Land had not been completely conquered, and, consequently, the Canaanites, led by King Jabin, were deadly foes. They lived during what is now called the Iron Age, and the people had capitalized on the art of using metal. They had hundreds of iron chariots against which the Hebrews had no defense. God was intensely disappointed with the corruption of His people, for even the ministry of judges did not abolish idolatry. The ancient writer said:

> And it came to pass, when the judge was dead, that they returned, and corrupted themselves more than their fathers, in following other gods to serve them, and to bow down unto them; they ceased not from their own doings, nor from their stubborn way (Judg. 2:19).

Deborah—The Magistrate . . . *Strange*

When the problems of administering justice became too strenuous, Moses, the patriarch, accepted the advice of his father-in-law and delegated duties to a special panel of judges (see Exod. 18:13–27). If for any reason they could not solve a problem, it was transferred to a Supreme Court. It was surprising when God chose a woman to be one of the judges; all other appointees were men. God raised Deborah to prominence and imparted the wisdom necessary for the performance of her duties. It was amazing that argumentative men were willing to accept her decisions. She expressed her views and had the courage to uphold and enforce her verdicts. It cannot be overemphasized that men, who probably disliked and disdained females, accepted the rulings of this official. They listened to her reasoning and sometimes feared, for she possessed authority and could not be challenged. A woman had become the representative of the laws of God.

Today the Western world has been made aware of the inherent capabilities of women to reach any level of society. Ladies have become famous administrators, politicians, and surgeons. Some occupy the highest positions in government.

That which was almost unknown in antiquity has become commonplace. It is worthy of note that in some countries the age-old customs prevail, and millions of women are still enslaved by tradition. The Gospel of Jesus Christ has done more to emancipate females than anything else in existence. It teaches the so-called weaker sex was meant by God to be the cherished partners of men. Wise women recognize this fact and are grateful to the Savior who liberated them.

Deborah—The Messenger . . . *Startling*

The term "judge" referred to her judicial character and professional ability; her decisions affected people. The designation "prophetess" indicated she was inspired by the Almighty. Deborah was apparently the only woman of her generation who enjoyed that privilege. It may appear strange that other prophets such as Moses, David, Isaiah, Jeremiah, the ten minor prophets, and several men in the New Testament, bequeathed to posterity permanent records of their ministry. Yet no woman left a record of her work. This lady had the ability to predict things to come, and her accuracy astonished the nation.

Dr. Herbert Lockyer wrote: "We have the exceptional case of Deborah, one of the most remarkable women in the Bible: prophet, judge, ruler, warrior, poetess. Boldly she could say—

The inhabitants of the villages ceased, they ceased in Israel, until that I Deborah arose; that I arose a mother in Israel (Judg. 5:7).

"Genius and talent found her able and ready to meet her nation's emergency and peril, so she became the first woman leader of men; the first public woman of the Bible with a passionate patriotism achieving such a victory that the land had rest from war for forty years."[1]

Perhaps Deborah's fame as a prophetess had developed over several years. People knew that her predictions were reliable, and her reputation reached new proportions when she foretold the destruction of enemies who had oppressed the nation for decades. God may have used this remarkable lady because He could not find a man capable of doing her work. Males like to believe they are indispensable, but history has demonstrated that when the best of men failed, the Lord found women whose courage and wisdom superseded anything possessed by males.

Deborah—The Militant... *Skillful*

It is interesting to note that Barak, the commander in chief of Israel's armies, was residing at Kedesh-Naphtali, apparently indifferent to the danger confronting his nation. That Deborah thought it necessary to assume command of the situation indicates the general's reluctance to defend his country. The enemy had a fortified city near the plains of Esdraelon, and the plain provided space in which their iron chariots could operate. The comparatively small army of Israel was vastly outnumbered, and it was evident the defenders had no chance of victory. Barak's fear was evident when he said to the prophetess, "If thou wilt go with me, then I will go: but if thou wilt not go with me, then I will not go" (Judg. 4:8). Deborah replied, "I will surely go with thee: notwithstanding the journey that thou takest shall not be for thine honour; for the LORD shall sell Sisera into the hand of a woman" (Judg. 4:9). The ten thousand men under the command of Barak were drawn from the northern tribes of Israel, but they were apprehensive as they followed their leader to the battlefield. What happened afterward is best described by Flavius Josephus, the Jewish historian.

So Deborah sent for Barak, and bade him choose him out ten thousand young men to go against the enemy, because God had said that number was sufficient and promised them victory. But when Barak said that he would not be the general unless she would also go as a general with him, she had indignation at what he said, and replied, "Thou, O Barak, deliverest up meanly that authority which God hath given thee into the hand of a woman, and I do not reject it." So they collected ten thousand men, and men, and pitched their camp at mount Tabor, where, at the king's command, Sisera met them, and pitched his camp not far from the enemy; whereupon the Israelites, and Barak himself, were so affrighted at the multitude of those enemies, that they were resolved to march off had not Deborah retained them, and commanded them to fight the enemy that very day, for that they should conquer them, and God would be their assistance.

So the battle began; and when they were come to close fight, there came down from heaven a great storm, with a vast quantity of rain and hail, and the wind blew the rain in the face of the Canaanites, and so darkened their eyes, that their arrows and slings were of no advantage to them, nor would the coldness of the air permit the soldiers to make use of their swords; while this storm did not so much incommode the Israelites, because it came in their backs. They also took such courage, upon the apprehension that God was assisting them, that they fell upon the very midst of their enemies, and slew a great number of them; so that some of them fell by the Israelites, some fell by their own horses, which were put into disorder, and not a few were killed by their own chariots.[2]

Deborah—The Musician . . . *Superb*

Then sang Deborah and Barak the son of Ahinoam on that day, saying: Praise ye the LORD for the avenging of Israel, when the people willingly offered themselves . . . LORD, when thou wentest out of Seir; when thou marchedst out of the field of Edom, the earth trembled, and the heavens dropped, the clouds also dropped water (Judg. 5:1–4).

They fought from heaven; the stars in their courses fought against Sisera. The river of Kishon swept them away, that ancient river, the river Kishon. O my soul, thou hast trodden down strength. Then were the horsehoofs broken by the means of the pransings, the pransings of their mighty ones (Judg. 5:20–22).

36

Four facets of Deborah's life and work shine as stars against the blackness of her surroundings. They are *her concern, consecration, courage,* and *composition.* They deserve investigation.

Her Concern

It is not known how this delightful woman became involved in Israel's legal system, but evidently her capabilities had been recognized by peers. She could have been as other women, a homemaker or a laborer in her husband's fields. The judge was scholarly and liked helping people with problems. Her decisions helped other women to obtain what otherwise might have been denied.

Her Consecration

Deborah's life had been surrendered to the Almighty, who blessed her with the spirit of prophecy. God used her intellectual capabilities, and when predictions were fulfilled, people in the vicinity began to appreciate her talent. This consecrated woman and the Almighty shared their lives. He inspired her, and she did the same for those who attended her court.

Her Confidence

When most of the inhabitants were overwhelmed by fear and invasions resulted in loss of life and property, this lady was alone. She summoned a frightened army commander and strengthened the hopes of an oppressed nation. Later, when many soldiers were tempted to run away, the unshaken faith of Deborah revived their spirits and made possible one of the greatest victories in military history. It is easy to visualize her standing in the devastating storm, gazing up into heaven, and praising God. The Lord is always invincible, but when a woman of this type is on His side, He must be delighted.

Her Composition

Poets, lyricists, and musicians are special people. They express the inexpressible and see things which only the supernatural can provide. Poetry is the music of the soul, a language which everybody understands. It captivates the glory of the eternal, embraces human need, and brings to the surface treasures only found in the depth of human consciousness. Deborah was one of those rare women who inspire everybody.

When the battle ended, she and her colleague sang the only mixed duet mentioned in the Scriptures. It revealed the surging emotions of two happy warriors. The reference to divine assistance was unmistakable. Torrential rain had flooded the plain; the river had overflowed its banks, and "the dropping heavens" evidently referred to atmospheric disturbances. The noise of thunder seemed to suggest heaven's armies were using heavy armament, and flashing lightning struck terror to horses attached to the chariots of iron. When the animals reared on their hind legs they began smashing everything within reach. The warriors were filled with confusion. Chariots were sinking in mud. As panic spread, soldiers began killing their comrades. To make matters worse, the ten thousand men of Israel began attacking, and it became evident the Syrians and Canaanites were doomed. The thunder in the heavens seemed to be applauding the victory. With despair filling his soul, Sisera, the general, fled. It was a remarkable day in Israel, and when Deborah and Barak began to sing, perhaps every soldier cheered. This remarkable woman was the proverbial Jack or Jill of all trades; she was the greatest lady in Israel. She would have loved Paul's statement: "If God be for us, who can be against us?" (Rom. 8:31).

1. Herbert Lockyer, *All the Kings and Queens of the Bible* (Grand Rapids: Zondervan Publishing House, 1988).

2. *The Complete Works of Flavius Josephus*, ed. William Whiston (Grand Rapids: Kregel Publications, 1979).

*And so it was, when Israel had sown, that the Midianites
came up, and the Amalekites, and the children of the east,
even they came up against them. And they encamped against
them, and destroyed the increase of the earth, till thou come
unto Gaza, and left no sustenance for Israel, neither sheep,
nor ox, nor ass. For they came up with their cattle and their
tents, and they came as grasshoppers for multitude; for both
they and their camels were without number: and they
entered into the land to destroy it. And Israel
was greatly impoverished (Judg. 6:3–6).*

The period when the children of Israel were ruled by judges
was probably the most distressing time in the history of the
Hebrew nation. The people had no permanent leader, no
standing army, nor discipline. Men did what they desired and
observed no law. At harvest time crops were destroyed by
unscrupulous invaders, homes were burned, and the people
were forced to live in mountain caves. The nation was greatly
impoverished. The exploits of Gideon may be summarized
under five headings.

Awestricken by an Angel

And there came an angel of the LORD, and sat under an oak
which was in Ophrah, that pertained unto Joash the Abiezrite:
and his son Gideon threshed wheat by the winepress, to hide
it from the Midianites. And the angel of the LORD appeared
unto him, and said unto him, The LORD is with three, thou
mighty man of valour (Judg. 6:11–12).

The plight of Gideon's family was terrible, and it was at
great risk the young man endeavored to make enough bread
to sustain them through the winter. He descended from a cave
in the mountains to thresh wheat, hoping he would be able to
save at least a portion of the crop before the arrival of the
dreaded invaders. When he saw an angel sitting beneath an
oak tree and later witnessed the miracle that consumed an

offering upon a nearby rock, Gideon trembled and said, "Alas, O Lord GOD! for because I have seen an angel of the LORD face to face" (Judg. 6:22). It was evident that God saw in him qualities which had never been recognized. When Gideon was instructed to destroy the family idol, he became very afraid, but, accompanied by some of his servants, he did as he was directed. "He could not do it by day, that he did it by night" (Judg. 6:27). As conditions within the community deteriorated, THE SPIRIT OF THE LORD CAME UPON GIDEON, and a comparative dwarf was transformed into a giant!

Amazed by an Answer

And Gideon said unto God, If thou wilt save Israel by my hand, as thou hast said, Behold, I will put a fleece of wool in the floor; and if the dew be on the fleece only, and it be dry upon all the earth beside, then shall I know that thou wilt save Israel by mine hand, as thou hast said (Judg. 6:36–37).

It is reassuring to know that God understands the frailty of His children and remembers that even the best of them are dust. Gideon had difficulty in believing he was to become a military leader and asked for signs to confirm what had been promised. When he put out a fleece and requested the Lord to perform a miracle, God did as He was asked. When Gideon desired a second miracle, the patience of the Almighty never faltered (see Judg. 6:39). Yet the testing of the man's faith continued. His army numbered 32,000 men, but when 22,000 of them confessed they were afraid and returned to their homes, Gideon trembled, for the enemy forces were as numerous as grasshoppers. When God announced the small army needed to be reduced even more, everybody wondered what was happening. Finally the leader was left with three hundred men, and apparently defeat was inevitable. Gideon looked at the equipment that consisted mainly of trumpets, pitchers, and lamps and thought his crusade to be suicidal.

It became evident to the ancient leader that God had no objection to being challenged. When he placed a fleece on the ground and asked that it would become wet with dew while

40

the earth remained dry, it appeared he was seeking a miracle. Did the Lord smile when he heard the request? Poor Gideon! Had he forgotten that the Almighty had made both the fleece and the ground upon which it was placed? It is difficult to understand why it was necessary for the man to make a second request. Perhaps he wanted to be sure! Other benefactors might have resented the renewed petition, saying, "Isn't he satisfied? What more does he require?" God understood the anxiety of His servant and graciously granted his requests. The fleece remained dry while the earth was saturated with moisture. Gideon was a very wise man; many of his successors went ahead with their own plans assuming the Lord would endorse their decisions. It is wiser to seek the guidance of God first than to wait until impetuosity leads to disaster.

Assured by an Alien

And it came to pass the same night, that the LORD said unto him, Arise, get thee down unto the host; for I have delivered it into thy hand. But if thou fear to go down, go thou with Phurah thy servant down to the host (Judg. 7:9–10).

When the Lord saw that Gideon was afraid, He told him he could take a companion on the mission. As they crouched together in the darkness, they overheard two Midianites discussing a dream. Gideon's faith was immediately strengthened, proving that, with every emergency, the Lord supplied new grace. Even in those days God was expressing a truth Paul described centuries later. "*God is faithful*, who will not suffer you to be tempted above that ye are able; but will with the temptation also make a way to escape, that ye may be able to bear it" (1 Cor. 10:13).

I remember when I was a child in Wales, my mother kept chickens in the yard close to our home. She enclosed the area with wire and in the top section had red birds and in the lower part, white ones. Surrounded by hens, the cockerels were like kings. I was interested to see the two male birds spend their time facing each other beak-to-beak as they paraded along their side of the wire netting. As a child of five years I watched

41

their antics and realized they hated each other. I asked my mother to open the door so that they could have a real fight. She was horrified and replied, "Son, I cannot do that. Those two birds cannot live together. One of them would kill the other." I was hoping to see a real battle, but my parent would not cooperate. I have since recognized those birds in other areas of life. Faith and Fear cannot live together. One will kill the other.

The heart of Gideon resembled, so to speak, my mother's garden. He knew both fear and faith, but it was quite a while before faith destroyed his unbelief. Nonetheless, the Lord never lost patience with His servant, and ultimately the enemy was vanquished.

Assisted by the Almighty

And the three hundred blew the trumpets, and the LORD set every man's sword against his fellow, even throughout all the host, and the host fled . . . And the men of Israel gathered themselves together . . . and pursued after the Midianites (Judg. 7:22–23).

"The ancient Israelites divided the night into three four-hour watches lasting from sunset to sunrise; that is from 6 P.M. until 6 A.M. The first watch is not mentioned in the Old Testament. According to this, Gideon's attack must have taken place soon after 10 P.M. or toward eleven. Later generations of Hebrews adopted the Roman division of four watches."[1]

The night was very dark, and assured of their safety, the Midianites were sleeping. It was approaching night when Gideon divided his 300 men into three companies and placed them strategically around the enemy encampment. Probably each man was armed with a shield and sword, but their main equipment consisted of a bugle and a pitcher which contained a lighted lamp. At the prearranged signal the pitchers were shattered and the trumpets blown, and the result was devastating. Aroused from their sleep by the thunderous crashing and piercing bugle calls, the bewildered men stared into the darkness to see hundreds of lights in all directions. Believing they were about to be attacked, they imagined their comrades to be enemies and began killing each other. The Lord took advantage of the situation, and within a short time, utterly confused, the Midianites were running for their lives. Pandemonium filled the camp, and before the Hebrews could strike a blow, the battle was won. When Gideon surveyed the battlefield, he remembered that God had said: "The people that are with thee are too many for me to give the Midianites into their hands, lest Israel vaunt themselves against me, saying, *mine own hand hath saved me*" (Judg. 7:2). Had it been necessary, Jehovah could have destroyed His foes without receiving help from anyone. He permitted a small company of men to participate in the conflict, to teach the entire nation that victory is assured "Not by might, nor by power, but by my spirit, saith the Lord of hosts" (see Zech. 4:6). The safest way to overcome a foe is to follow the guidance of God. His soldiers may suffer temporary setbacks, but they cannot lose the war!

Attracted by Articles

And Gideon said unto them, I would desire a request of you, that ye would give me every man the earrings of his prey. (They had golden earrings because they were Ishmaelites.) And they answered, We will willingly give them. And they spread a garment, and did cast therein every man the earrings of his prey. And the weight of the golden earrings that he requested was a thousand and seven hundred shekels of gold; beside ornaments and collars, and purple raiment that was on the kings of Midian, and beside the chains that were about their camels' necks (Judg. 8:24–26).

Gideon was one of the outstanding characters mentioned in the Old Testament, but it must be remembered he was only human. His attraction for jewelry destroyed his integrity. He had been an impoverished man trying to survive Midianite aggression. Yet afterward he lived and died as a king. His fame was established when he became God's associate. His fortune was assured when he received the wealth scattered over a battlefield. The ancient Ishmaelites from whom the Midianites descended adorned themselves with golden necklaces and earrings, and even their camels were decorated with golden chains. When thousands of their soldiers lay dead upon the battlefield, an immense treasure awaited the conquerors. Gideon knew this, and the opportunity to become wealthy was irresistible. He asked for compensation, and the people agreed to give him the earrings and chains formerly possessed by the enemy. These were placed on a garment spread upon the ground. With his wealth Gideon built a shrine in the city of Ophrah, where he placed an ephod such as was worn by the high priest of Israel. Doubtless this was meant to be a reminder of the victory over the Midianites, but unfortunately, "all Israel went thither a whoring after it: which thing became a snare unto Gideon, and to his house. . . . And the country was in quietness forty years in the days of Gideon" (Judg. 8:27–28). "And Gideon the son of Joash died in a good old age, and was buried in the sepulchre of Joash his father, in Ophrah of the Abiezrites" (Judg. 8:32).

It is extremely difficult to understand how this great man of God could worship idols. Evidently the love of money affected his heart, and his association with idolaters polluted his mind. His story provides a warning for every child of God. As long as Gideon listened to the Lord, he was safe. When he lost that intimate fellowship and pandered to base desires, he lost his serenity. He conquered the Midianites but lost the conflict against himself.

1. *The Pulpit Commentary*, vol. 3 (Peabody, Mass.:Hendrickson Publishers, 1984).

And the messenger answered and said, Israel is fled before the Philistines, and there hath also been a great slaughter among the people, and thy two sons also, Hophni and Phinehas, are dead, and the ark of God is taken. And it came to pass, when he made mention of the ark of God, that he [Eli] fell from off his seat backward by the side of the gate, and his neck brake, and he died: for he was an old man, and heavy. And he had judged Israel forty years (1 Sam. 4:17–18).

Eli, the high priest at Shiloh, resembled a very tall tree in a forest. He was destroyed, not by a tempest, but by decay which worked from within. When at the age of ninety-eight he fell from a bench at the city gate, it was the climax of a long process that had threatened him for many years. The unwise old prelate should have resigned his office much earlier, but he was the classic example of a man who expected other people to follow precepts which he ignored. The cancer that he neglected killed him. His heart was broken long before his neck.

Eli's Commitment . . . *Consecration*

And the holy garments of Aaron shall be his sons' after him, to be anointed therein, and to be consecrated in them. And that son that is priest in his stead shall put them on seven days, when he cometh into the tabernacle of the congregation to minister in the holy place (Exod. 29:29–30).

To become a servant of the Lord was one of the greatest privileges bestowed upon a man. To be chosen as the high priest of the nation was even more important, for that individual became God's representative upon the earth. There is every reason to believe that when Eli was ordained, he was all the Lord desired. This kind of man is always worthy of applause, but the position carries enormous responsibility. The priest was also the judge of Israel, and such men were not expected

to have favorites or be biased in making decisions. To stand
tall in the service of the Almighty is something to be desired,
but when one of God's trusted servants dishonors his calling,
it is an occasion for intense regret. As Eli increased in age, his
two sons took over his duties and brought dishonor to their
profession. The doting father failed to control them, and the
situation became deplorable.

Eli's inability to influence his sons made him irritable and
hasty. His treatment of Hannah, a woman he saw praying in
the sanctuary, left much to be desired. The priest, who should
have been cautious, understanding, and kind, embarrassed an
innocent lady. That the man changed his opinion did not ease
the pain she had already endured. Eli did more damage in
moments than he could repair in months. That was not per-
missible in the conduct of anyone who represented the Lord.

Eli's Conduct... *Callous*

When Eli died at the age of ninety-eight, he had ruled the
nation for forty years. People came to him from all directions
to seek a solution to their problems. He usually sat on a bench
close to the city gate, and therefore it was not difficult for
strangers to obtain an audience with the prelate. One day he
saw Hannah, the wife of Elkanah, and unfortunately made
one of his greatest mistakes. The childless woman was ear-
nestly asking Jehovah to grant her a son. Among her neighbors she was considered accursed, and this, when added to the
contempt shown by Elkanah's second wife, produced a burden too heavy to carry. Filled with grief and desire, she prayed
in the temple precincts. Her lips moved but her silent petition
arose from the depths of a troubled soul. Eli heard no sound
and concluded she was one of the drunken prostitutes who
frequented the house of God. It is said that "he marked her
mouth." Some people might believe the priest struck her, but
possibly he only noticed the movement of her lips; her voice
was unheard. Eli knew evil women existed, for his own sons
fraternized with them. The old priest knew exactly what was
happening but was too weak to remove his sons from office.
He had tolerated this situation for years and condoned the evil

practices. The elderly prelate failed to detect the difference between immoral people and a true worshiper. It was an amazing fact that God's grace had permitted his ministry to extend over so many years; he was unfit for duty.

Probably the Almighty was waiting for Samuel to become the new leader of Israel. God, who sees the end from the beginning, is an expert preparing for eventualities. It is sad to relate that when a man tolerates sin, his sensitivity diminishes.

Eli's Child . . . *Called*

> And when she had weaned him [Samuel] . . . she . . . brought the child to Eli. And she said, Oh my lord, as thy soul liveth, my lord, I am the woman that stood by thee here, praying unto the LORD. For this child I prayed; and the LORD hath given me my petition which I asked of him. Therefore also I have lent him to the LORD; as long as he liveth he shall be lent to the LORD. And he worshiped the LORD there (1 Sam. 1:24–28).

Her sacrificial gift cannot be underestimated; she surrendered her only child and had no assurance of giving birth again. The kindness of God was extended, for the Scriptures say, "the LORD visited Hannah, so that she conceived, and bare three sons and two daughters" (1 Sam. 2:21). God has always known how to pay His debts!

How the elderly priest coped with the varying needs of the small child can only be assumed. Possibly he enlisted the services of one of the dedicated women associated with the sanctuary (compare Luke 2:36–37). As Samuel developed, the impact upon his clerical guardian must have been tremendous. The boy's purity of soul and blessed simplicity reminded Eli of earlier days and at the same time aroused premonitions that his own ministry was terminating. This assurance was increased when Jehovah called the boy in the night, and Eli had to explain the significance of the voice heard in the darkness. To his credit it should be remembered that during these trying experiences, the priest remained faithful to his youthful protégé.

Many years later when King Herod heard of a Child who

would become the ruler of Israel, he became infuriated and ordered the execution of every baby within his domain. Eli was more gracious; he taught and protected Samuel who eventually became his successor.

Eli's Children... *Criminal*

Jehovah made ample provision for the support of his ministers, but the sons of Levi were dissatisfied with that arrangement. They were more concerned with feeding their stomachs than filling their sanctuary. Their threats brought chaos to the temple services and disgust to the nation. The ancient writer described how their behavior aroused anger throughout the nation (see 1 Sam. 2:13–17). When Eli condemned his sons for associating with prostitutes who operated close to the tabernacle precincts, his remonstration was as ineffective as a gentle tap on the hand. The old man, who might have been as dynamic as Moses, was a reed shaken by the wind. When his sons ignored his advice, they signed their death warrants.

> Wherefore the sin of the young men was very great before the LORD; for men abhorred the offering of the LORD (1 Sam. 2:17).

Had Eli done his duty, the people of Israel would have applauded his actions and supported his endeavor. Unfortunately, he had become an object of scorn and completely unfit to be the high priest. This story from antiquity indicates the higher a man climbs, the greater may be his fall. It gives warning to everyone who thinks he stands, to take heed lest he fall. A career that has taken a lifetime to establish can be destroyed in moments.

Eli's Collapse... *Complete*

And the man said unto Eli, I am he that came out of the army, and I fled today out of the army. And he said, What is there done, my son? And the messenger answered and said, Israel is fled before the Philistines, and there hath been also a great slaughter among the people, and thy two sons also, Hophni and Phinehas, are dead, and the ark of God is taken. And it came to pass, when he made mention of the ark of God, that he [Eli] fell from off the seat backward by the side of the gate, and his neck brake, and he died: for he was an old man and heavy (1 Sam. 4:16–18).

"Now Eli was ninety and eight years old; and his eyes were dim, that he could not see" (1 Sam. 4:15). The messenger who informed the priest about the outcome of the battle with the Philistines mentioned three calamities. (1) There had been a great slaughter among the people, (2) Eli's sons were dead, and (3) the sacred ark had been captured by the enemy. It was significant that Israel's defeat and the death of the two sons were unimportant compared with the loss of the ark. When Eli heard of the terrible catastrophe, he lost his composure, overbalanced, and fell from his bench. The weight of his heavy body fell on the neck of the priest, and it snapped. It might be concluded that the cause of death was a broken neck, but in the final analysis, Eli was dead before he died. Eli had lost fellowship with Jehovah, the respect of the nation, and at ninety-eight years of age had nothing for which to live. The old priest had no mourners at his funeral. The people believed they were better off without him.

It is always a cause for sorrow when one of God's chosen instruments falls from grace. Such an event invites criticism from watching unbelievers. Eli had lived in fellowship with God; he should have known better. His piety was undermined by compromise. When he spared his sons, he destroyed himself!

And the child Samuel grew on, and was in favour both with the LORD, and also with men (1 Sam. 2:26).

The forces of evil may appear to win occasional battles, but the final victory belongs to God. When Moses failed, Joshua took his place. When Eli disappointed the Lord, Samuel was already being prepared. When Elijah was scared by Jezebel and lost his influence over Israel, the Lord commissioned a young man called Elisha, whose magnificent ministry saved the nation. After the betrayal by Judas, Paul appeared from nowhere to become the greatest evangelist ever known by the church. Often excessive admiration of a man leads to disappointment, but "Whoso putteth his trust in the LORD shall be safe" (Prov. 29:25).

My wife and I have traveled extensively throughout Europe and have admired the magnificent architecture of many ornate Cathedrals. St. Peter's, in Vatican City, is a lofty, historic structure. The Cathedral of Notre Dame is an amazing building, but in my estimation no sanctuary is more attractive than the Cathedral at Milan. I cannot forget gazing at the triple archway of its main entrance. Long ago the stone cutter engraved for posterity a most important truth. He carved over one arch a wreath of roses and placed underneath: "All that pleases is but for a moment." Over the other arch he carved a cross and the words: "All that troubles is but for a moment." Finally, above the main entrance he chiseled: "That only is important which is eternal."

Only one life, 'twill soon be past;
Only what's done for Christ will last.

THE NAMELESS CHILD FROM ISRAEL

Now Naaman, captain of the host of the king of Syria, was a
great man with his master, and honourable, because by him
the LORD had given deliverance unto Syria: he was also a
mighty man in valour, but he was a leper. And the Syrians
had gone out by companies, and had brought away captive
out of the land of Israel a little maid; and she waited on
Naaman's wife (2 Kings 5:1–2).

If I were the pastor of a church, I would prepare a series of
sermons about the nameless characters mentioned in the Bible.
It is interesting to note that some of the most important events
in Jewish history featured people whose names remain
unknown. Among the many that could be studied is the maid
who was captured during one of the raids on Israel. This
insignificant child became a servant in the household of
Naaman, the commander in chief of the Syrian armies. She
resembled a very small spring that gave birth to a river of
divine benediction. The story begins with the statement.

The northern border of Israel was always a place of danger.
Even today raiders from Lebanon and Syria attack the villages
occupied by Jewish settlers, and the young Hebrews plow
fields and carry guns at the same time. Great efforts are being
made to establish peace in the area, but the retaliation of Arab
extremists continues to cause international concern. Little has
changed since the times when ancient Syrians terrorized the
inhabitants of northern Palestine. The story of this unnamed
Jewish girl began in that depressing period. The writer of this
narrative was content to say: "And the Syrians had gone out
by companies and had brought away captive out of the land of
Israel a little maid; and she waited on Naaman's wife."

The Hebrews were formidable defenders, and the attack by
their enemies was probably made under cover of darkness.
Maybe the girl was awakened by the screams of dying
neighbors, and while she sat paralyzed by fear, a stranger
burst into her bedroom and dragged her from the house. All
around was evidence of the brutality of the attack and perhaps

her parents lay dead on the ground. That night the child lost everything she valued. Within a few minutes her parents, friends, and all she loved disappeared forever. Devastated by shock and grief, the maiden was compelled to accompany her captor as the Syrian invaders returned to their own land. It is unlikely that Naaman, the commander in chief, had taken part in actual combat. Since the record states "The Syrians" had carried away the captive, Dr. Herbert Lockyer may be correct when he suggests she was seized by a soldier and later offered for sale in the slave market in Damascus. Perhaps Naaman saw the girl as they returned from the raid and purchased her then or even accepted her as a trophy of his victory. Some details were not supplied by the ancient author who was content to say: "She waited on Naaman's wife."

It is not difficult to imagine the terror with which the child began her new life. She was among strangers whom she had every reason to hate. If she were offered for sale in the Damascus slave market, the possibility of a life of shame threatened her future. The girl was without hope in an alien land. The home of Syria's greatest soldier was probably a pretentious palace and very different from the primitive hut in which she had been reared. The smiles of her mistress may have reassured the child, and the new clothing in which she was soon attired restored calm to her troubled mind. It is edifying to consider this little-big girl from Israel.

Her Scintillating Fortitude... *Astonishing*

The fact that this maiden lost everything except her faith in God suggests she was reared in a devout family who instructed her in the laws of Jehovah. It is a cause for amazement that the terrible tragedy that overwhelmed the village failed to destroy her faith. The instruction received from childhood survived the storm that changed her life. In common with the stars of heaven, her light was seen more clearly in darkness. When the maid became aware of Naaman's illness and saw the concern on the face of her mistress, she said, "Would God my lord were with the prophet that is in Samaria, for he would recover him of his leprosy" (2 Kings 5:3).

I lived through two world wars when bombs fell upon innumerable homes in Wales. Unfortunately, people could not understand why God did nothing to protect them from adversity. Many homes were destroyed, and distressed people criticized the Lord for not preventing the tragedy. When danger threatened, the churches were filled with praying people. It was disappointing when at the end of the war multitudes celebrated the victory by getting drunk. Churches had smaller congregations, while taverns were too small to accommodate customers. It is refreshing to see this child from Israel against the disappointing background of human ingratitude. The girl from a bygone age lost everything except her indestructible faith in God.

Her Sublime Faith . . . *Abiding*

There is no evidence to prove the captive ever saw the prophet Elisha and no reason to believe she had witnessed the cleansing of a leper. Her faith was probably the product of early instruction. The young Hebrew had reason to hate the general who organized the raid on her village. Many Jews would have rejoiced that sickness had undermined the health of their adversary and would have welcomed his death. The idea of loving enemies was unknown. The Syrian deserved to die; he was responsible for the death of many innocent people. The law said: "An eye for an eye, and a tooth for a tooth," and that same precept confirmed the Jews' opinion— "A life for a life." Every person in Israel rejoiced over the misfortune of their archenemy. There was also another reason why they disliked the foreigner; he was a Gentile who had no place in their religion and was an enemy of Jehovah.

The captive maid refused to accept such ideas, and it is therefore difficult to overestimate the worth of her character. Her master needed help, and she believed it was the duty of everyone to render assistance when and where it was needed. The girl refused to permit prejudice to taint her soul; she believed the God of Israel would welcome anyone who came to Him. Faith and compassion should destroy all barriers dividing the nations of the world. It has always been better to lift a man up and make a friend, than to strike a man down and create an enemy. If the modern world emulated the example set by the ancient maiden, wars would be unknown; pain and sickness, removed eternally; and the earth would become an extension of heaven. Did Isaiah have this thought in mind when he wrote: "And a little child shall lead them?" (see Isa. 11:6).

Her Sincere Friendship . . . *Admirable*

When the girl from Israel began her service in Naaman's household, she became concerned about the health of her master. When she saw worry showing on the face of her mistress she was troubled even more. Evidently Naaman's leprosy was either in its early stages, or was one of the less dangerous varieties of the disease. The future was ominous, and each time the great soldier went to war his wife wondered which would kill her husband—leprosy or his foes. He was famous for his bravery, but this sickness was an invincible foe. Everybody in Syria admired his tremendous courage but all expected his imminent death. The problem was a cloud of apprehension hovering over the entire country.

One day her mistress probably asked, "Are you ill?" "No, Mistress." "Well, something is bothering you. Are you not happy among us?" "Oh, yes, you have been very kind to me." "Then why are you sad?" The girl hesitated for a moment, and then replied, "I am worried about the master." "Yes, we are all troubled." The maid then said, "If only he were with the prophet in Samaria; the man of God would cleanse him from this leprosy. I know he would." When the Syrian lady asked for an explanation, she was told of the exploits of Elisha, who could perform miracles. He was not a physician but was God's servant capable of doing anything he desired. The mistress became excited and shared her information with an unknown friend from the royal household.

Hearing the good news, the king of Syria summoned Naaman and commended him to leave immediately for Samaria. He promised to write a letter to the ruler of Israel commanding him to assist his special friend. When the king of Israel read that message, he became terrified, suspecting it to be an excuse for another raid upon his people. Angrily he exclaimed:

Am I God, to kill and to make alive, that this man doth send unto me to recover a man of his leprosy? Wherefore consider, I pray you, how he seeketh a quarrel against me (2 Kings 5:7).

The frightened man became so enraged that he panicked and tore his garments to shreds. Even now it is strange to contrast the faith of a young girl with the fear of the king who ruled the nation! Evidently, the child was closer to God than the king she was expected to honor. She resembled David, who scoffed at Goliath while Saul and his army remained paralyzed by fear. That young lady would have made an excellent queen for David, but alas, she belonged to a different age. The servant exhibited the characteristics described by Paul to be the fruit of the Spirit (see Gal. 5:22 and Eph. 4:31–32). If we may describe the circumstances that led to the cleansing of Naaman as a chain, then this compassionate child from Israel was its first link. Her mistress, the person who repeated the news to the king, and the soldier who defied the general's anger, were also unnamed heroes who helped to save Naaman's life.

When the leper arrived at Elisha's cottage, he expected to be welcomed with honors usually given to visiting dignitaries. He was insulted and irritated when he was received as a commoner. His rage was evident, his face livid with anger, and his denunciations were unmistakable. The idea of asking a general to bathe in the river Jordan was outrageous. He shouted:

Are not Abana and Pharpar, rivers of Damascus better than all the waters of Israel? May I not wash in them, and be clean? (2 Kings 5:12).

Fear, anxiety, and hope had occupied his thought as he journeyed from Syria, but when he was treated with apparent disrespect, his soul erupted. It was an unnamed man who risked his future and life when he accused Naaman of being unreasonable. Proud men dislike rebukes. The subordinate said, "Master, if that prophet had commanded you to fight twenty men half of them would have been already dead. You would have demonstrated how great a warrior you are. But, Sir, there is no need to prove anything; we know how courageous you have always been. Master, you only need to demonstrate your ability to take orders even as we do. . . . How much rather then when he saith unto thee, Wash and be clean."

Her Surprising Fame . . . *Amazing*

Sometimes it is not the prominent figures in a painting that captivate attention. The details in the background sometimes reveal the artist's ability. That was evident in this scene from antiquity. The eminent commander by whom deliverance had been given to Syria, the monarch who sent him to seek cleansing in Israel, and the prophet of God were very important in the divine plan. Nevertheless, without the nameless maid, the wife and the messenger who repeated the girl's message to the king, and the soldier who challenged his furious commander, God's historic picture would have been incomplete.

The moral of this story is easily understood. When God makes a chain of circumstances, He uses many links which by themselves would be useless. There are many preachers whose eloquence thrills great congregations, talented singers whose music enthralls an audience, but there are multitudes of "small" people who are just as precious in the Lord's sight. No task is insignificant when performed for the glory of Christ. He is able to take unimportant details and weave them into a pattern of extreme beauty. I have always admired Persian rugs, but one stitch never made a carpet. Many threads make a pattern, and under the skilled supervision of the craftsman, the design ultimately becomes an object of great beauty. When we arrive in God's country, we may discover that insignificant acts on earth were used by God to produce amazing results!

EZRA—WHO CARRIED GOLD
THROUGH A LAND OF BANDITS

And we came to Jerusalem, and abode there three days. Now on the fourth day was the silver and the gold and the vessels weighed in the house of our God by the hand of Memeroth the son of Uriah the priest . . . By number and by weight of every one: and all the weight was written at that time (Ezra 8:32–34).

Ezra was a scribe employed by the kings of Babylon and Persia. He lived in an age when the art of printing was unknown. The first writing was made on either clay tablets or engraved by masons on monumental columns. Important messages were written by hand, and consequently, scribes were valuable assets in any community. Ezra was known to three royal families, and became the messenger between the kings of Babylon and the Hebrews rebuilding Jerusalem.

When Cyrus conquered Babylon, he ordered the repatriation of all slaves. A vast expedition was arranged which included nearly fifty thousand people, 736 horses, 245 mules, 435 camels, and 6,720 donkeys (see Ezra 2:64–67). This caravan led by Nehemiah reached Jerusalem, and the work of reconstruction commenced. Certain Gentiles desired to assist in the building but were refused because they were aliens. Infuriated, they decided to oppose the builders, and part of their strategy was the writing of malicious letters to the Babylon monarchs who were chief sponsors of the project (see Ezra 4:4–24). It was at this point in history that Ezra appeared (see Ezra 7:1).

His research persuaded Artaxerxes that the letter he received was untrue. The Jews whom he had helped were loyal friends and deserved better treatment. He immediately rescinded his former decision, and increased his assistance to the Hebrews. Ezra was not only instructed to send another letter to Jerusalem—he was commissioned to lead a second expedition to supply everything necessary for the completion of the project. The details recorded by the industrious scribe were written in the book bearing his name. It was at that time Ezra faced his greatest challenge. Between Babylon and Jerusalem were hundreds of miles of desert that provided cover for bandits. Ezra realized he had no army to protect the enormous treasure to be carried to Jerusalem. The many males in the first expedition had guaranteed the safety of all concerned, but a smaller company would be in jeopardy. Four months of hazardous pilgrimage lay ahead, and danger was inescapable.

Ezra's Commission . . . *Chosen*

Artaxerxes, king of kings, unto Ezra the priest, a scribe of the law of the God of heaven, perfect peace, and at such a time. I make a decree, that all they of the people of Israel, and of his priests and Levites, in my realm, which are minded of their own freewill to go up to Jerusalem, go with thee. Forasmuch as thou art sent of the king, and of his seven counsellors, to enquire concerning Judah and Jerusalem (Ezra 7:12–14).

Ezra was a man who came from comparative obscurity to become one of the greatest men in Hebrew history. He was a priest, a scribe, a researcher, a person whom God and the king trusted. The accusing letter sent by pagans in Palestine annoyed the king, who threatened to deprive the Jews of necessary assistance. The people who were restoring Jerusalem had no defender, and when everything seemed to be lost, Ezra changed the course of history. He was appointed to lead a new expedition to deliver necessary supplies for the success of the reconstruction. The task was frightening, for the caravan train would attract the attention of every thief in the desert (see Ezra 7:9).

This priest apparently had no military experience. He was a scribe. Why the king appointed this inexperienced man to lead such an expedition can only be surmised. Ezra must have been an extraordinary man.

Ezra's Concern . . . *Conscientious*

Then I proclaimed a fast there, at the river of Ahava, that we might afflict ourselves before our God, to seek of him a right way for us, and for our little ones, and for all our substance. For I was ashamed to require of the king a band of soldiers and horsemen to help us against the enemy in the way: because we had spoken unto the king, saying, The hand of our God is upon all them for good that seek him; but his power and his wrath is against all them that forsake him (Ezra 8:21–22).

This was Ezra's finest hour. The people were ready to begin their journey, the vast treasure had been packed in crates, the herds of cattle were ready to move, but the priest was worried. He considered the difficult journey ahead and knew it was almost an impossibility to reach Jerusalem safely. The king who had financed the effort would be willing to supply an escort of soldiers, but the thoughtful leader considered that possibility and shook his head. How could he solicit aid when he had already assured the king Jehovah would help His people? The time had arrived when God should display His ability.

Today's religious leaders would have organized a telethon to raise enough money to pay for an escorting army. Ezra refused to beg, preferring to bow before the throne of grace. "So we fasted and besought our God for this: *and he was intreated of us*" (Ezra 8:23).

Ezra's Courage . . . *Commendable*

Then I separated twelve of the chief of the priests . . . and ten of their brethren with them. And weighed unto them the silver, and the gold, and the vessels, even the offering of the house of our God. . . . And I said unto them, Ye are holy unto the LORD; the vessels are holy also; and the silver and the gold are a freewill offering unto the LORD God of your fathers. Watch ye, and keep them until ye weigh them before the chief of the priests and the Levites, and chief of the fathers of Israel, at Jerusalem, in the chambers of the house of the LORD (Ezra 8:24–29).

It may have been significant that *after* the people had fasted and prayed, this industrious scribe summoned the priests and entrusted to their care the treasures which were to be transported to Jerusalem. Ezra probably realized that some of the gifts would be required for wages, materials, and other expenses, and was concerned that some of God's money might be used for other purposes. Long afterward the Savior said to His disciples: "But seek ye *first* the kingdom of God, and his righteousness; and all these things shall be added unto you" (Matt. 6:33). Ezra did what the Lord recommended. How he handled the finances of that expedition should be a model for every financial advisor. Everything of value was carefully weighed before witnesses, and a record was made for future reference. Ezra 8:32–34 supplies important information: "And we came to Jerusalem, and abode there three days. Now on the fourth day was the silver and the gold and the vessels weighed in the house of our God . . . by number and by weight of every one: and all the weight was written at that time." Ezra was a most meticulous treasurer. He avoided every possibility of theft, and even critics could not complain about the service rendered. Apparently the man received no payment for his work. If he controlled the finances of the United States of America, there would not be a deficit. This man was a financial wizard!

Ezra's Conquest . . . *Complete*

It must be considered amazing that such a genius for details refrained from supplying information concerning his long journey through the wilderness. The scribe who recorded even minor events confined his report to a few words:

Then we departed from the river of Ahava on the twelfth day of the first month, to go unto Jerusalem: and the hand of our God was upon us, and he delivered us from the hand of the enemy, and of such as lay in wait by the law. And we came to Jerusalem, and abode there three days (Ezra 8:31–32).

Evidently armed bandits tried to ambush the travelers, but as Ezra confessed, the hand of God protected the pilgrims, and they reached their destination safely. Probably the priestly author had to assume the post of commander in chief of the expedition, and what he lacked in military experience was supplied by his communion with God. He became the second in command, for as the Angel of the Lord came to assist Joshua (see Josh. 5:13–15), so He came to help the inexperienced Ezra. Nevertheless, it would be expected the ancient writer would say something about the spectacular events that occurred during the journey to Jerusalem. Was he afraid of the praise of men and determined Jehovah should have all the glory? It would appear this man from a bygone age not only conquered his enemies, he vanquished personal desires for fame or notoriety. He had been entrusted with a special task, and his only ambition was to fulfill his duties efficiently. Had he lived in a later age, he would have been able to say with Paul: "I live; yet not I, but Christ liveth in me" (see Gal. 2:20). The apostle John would have admired the ancient leader, for Ezra could have been a strange contrast to "Diotrephes, who loveth to have the preeminence" (see 3 John 9).

Ezra's Contribution... *Considerable*

Now therefore make confession unto the LORD God of your fathers, and do his pleasure: and separate yourselves from the people of the land, and from the strange wives. Then all the congregation answered and said with a loud voice, As thou hast said, so must we do (Ezra 10:11–12).

It became increasingly evident that the messenger from Babylon was held in the highest esteem by the Hebrew people. That they accepted his advice and obeyed his orders indicated he had won their esteem. He was a man who reached a pinnacle of excellence because he truly belonged to Jehovah. He and Nehemiah were among the most patriotic of all the Hebrews. They remain examples for all who desire to serve God. Ezra not only exhibited concern for God's work, he put muscles into his prayers and never expected others to work while he watched. His favorite text might have been: "Whatsoever thy hand findeth to do, *do it with thy might*" (Eccl. 9:10).

61

*When the morning stars sang together, and all the sons of
God shouted for joy (Job 38:7).*

And they sung a new song (Rev. 5:9).

There is a vast difference between music and noise, but
unfortunately some people do not appreciate the fact! Music
is attractive, soothing, and wonderful; noise is offensive, un-
appealing, and without merit. Webster's Dictionary defines
music as: "The art and science of combining vocal or instru-
mental sounds or tones in varying harmony or rhythm." If
music disappeared, the world would lose much of its charm.
It is almost frightening to remember that there was a time
when the earth was a place of silence. Then the Creator introduced the sigh of the wind in the trees, the song of a bird in
the forest, and the gentle murmurs of waves falling upon a
sandy beach. It took a longer period for man to learn how to
sing, but humans were eventually compelled to express their
happiness. Increasing pleasure does not live with silent tongues.
The first reference to music was made when God questioned
Job about the creation of the world. The Lord said, "Where
wast thou when I laid the foundations of the earth? . . . When
the morning stars sang together, and all the sons of God shouted
for joy?" (Job 38:4, 7). How that music eventually spread
through this world is an exciting story.

The Song of Redemption . . . *Gratitude*

Then sang Moses and the children of Israel this song unto the
Lord, and spake, saying, I will sing unto the Lord, for he
hath triumphed gloriously: the horse and his rider hath he
thrown into the sea (Exod. 15:1).

It may be significant that the earliest days of man were
shrouded in mystery. The descendants of Adam and Eve had
little to bequeath to their offspring. The ancient records say
men lived, begat children, and then died. This continued until

after the marriages of Lamech when the historian began supplying details of the talents possessed by individuals. For example, the children of Lamech and Adah became cattle-rearing nomads (Gen. 4:20). The family of their second son, Jubal, made and played harps and organs. A son born to his second wife, Zilla, was called Tubal-cain who became an instructor in the making of articles from brass and iron (see Gen. 4:22). It is interesting that the second son developed a love for musical instruments.

That gift became the heritage of God's people. When Jehovah rescued Israel from slavery in Egypt, Moses looked back over the watery grave of his enemies and led the Israelites in an anthem of praise.

> And Miriam the prophetess, the sister of Aaron, took a timbrel in her hand; and all the women went out after her with timbrels and with dances. And Miriam answered them, Sing ye to the LORD, for he hath triumphed gloriously; the horse and his rider hath he thrown into the sea (Exod. 15:20–21).

That spontaneous outburst of praise was the first celebration held among the people of God.

The Song Requested . . . *Gloom*

After the children of Israel returned from Babylon, one of their scribes wrote:

> By the rivers of Babylon, there we sat down, yea, we wept, when we remembered Zion. We hanged our harps upon the willows in the midst thereof. For there they that carried us away captive required of us a song; and they that wasted us required of us mirth, saying, Sing us one of the songs of Zion. How shall we sing the LORD's song in strange land? (Ps. 137:1–3).

It is thought-provoking that the request of the Babylonians was refused. It is always difficult for brokenhearted people to produce mirth. Music is always muted when the voice is hushed by sobs. Those Hebrews would have appreciated the message of a modern hymn:

> The peaceful hours I once enjoyed,
> How sweet the memory still;
> But they have left an aching, void
> The world can never fill.

The prisoners were troubled by unpleasant memories. This always happens when people lose God, their sanctuary, and never listen to a prophet. Daniel had risen to heights of distinction in Babylon, but he was never as confident as when he prayed before opened windows.

A tremendous transformation occurred when God rescued His suffering people. One of their number wrote: "When the LORD turned again the captivity of Zion, we were like them that dream. Then was our mouth filled with laughter, and our tongue with singing. Then said they among the heathen, The LORD hath done great things for them" (Ps. 126:1–2). When a believer has lost the peace which formerly filled his soul, he should retrace his steps and correct his mistake. When debris chokes a well, it is wise to remove the hindrance so that the springs may once again become active.

The Song of the Redeemer . . . *Gracious*

And when they had sung an hymn, they went out into the mount of Olives (Mark 14:26).

It is impossible to comprehend how the Savior could sing in the most difficult period of His life. He was suffering extreme anguish; His body was soon to be nailed to a cross when he would bear the sins of the world. Judas was planning to betray Him, and the other disciples would run for their lives. Yet, in spite of the unprecedented circumstances, Jesus completed the Passover Feast by singing a psalm normally used during the commemoration. It is difficult to understand His ability to do this when other people would have been devastated. It should be remembered what the writer to the

Hebrews said of the Lord: *"who for the joy that was set before him* endured the cross, despising the shame, and is set down at the right hand of the throne of God" (Heb. 12:2). The composure of Christ remained undisturbed because His fellowship with God was unbroken.

During the Savior's temptation in the wilderness, His ministry, and the awful sufferings that He endured, the Lord thought only of others. When the forces of evil would have overwhelmed Him, Christ was indeed "The Sun of righteousness, who arose with healing in His wings" (see Mal. 4:2). The music of victory was never silenced.

The Song of Rejoicing... *Gladness*

And at midnight Paul and Silas prayed, and sang praises unto God: and the prisoners heard them (Acts 16:25).

The city of Philippi was in an uproar; the citizens who were usually calm and restrained had become an infuriated mob. Two strangers had interfered with the lucrative business of a fortune teller, and her employers, realizing a valuable source of income had been lost, blamed the preachers. The magistrates who forgot their sacred duty of being just became a part of the unruly crowd. Bleeding and in danger of becoming martyrs, Paul and Silas were dragged through the city and thrown into prison. Their blood dripped on the dirty floor while pandemonium reigned in the streets. Then a voice was heard in the darkness: "Silas, are you awake?" "Yes, my brother, I am." "How do you feel?" "Well, I have felt better but thank God, I am alive." "Brother Silas, let's give them something to think about. Let's sing." Maybe their voices at first were not too resonant, but soon the prison echoed with glorious music. The other prisoners would normally have complained, but they realized this was something strange. The new inmates were either mad or remarkable people. When an earthquake increased the sounds in the night, most of the prisoners believed the world was falling apart. When the jailer discovered what had happened, Paul and Silas, fearing the man might injure himself, shouted, "Do thyself no harm, we are all here." That night was never forgotten. It was the only time men sang their way out of prison.

The Song of Reunion... *Glorious*

> And they sung a new song . . . And the number of them was ten thousand times ten thousand, and thousands of thousands, Saying with a loud voice, worthy is the lamb that was slain (Rev. 5:9–12).

The world has enjoyed the renditions of many massed choirs, for even the ancient Hebrews supported the choirs that sang in the tabernacle and temple. The Levites performed for specified periods before returning to their homes to enjoy short vacations. Throughout history nations arranged special celebrations of praise, and the wonderful choirs of Europe enthralled innumerable listeners. Kings, queens, and distinguished citizens have acclaimed the splendor of the magnificent performers. From the cathedrals of Europe to the valleys of Wales and beyond, music has been the highlight of every community. Even the birds greet the dawn with an anthem of praise. Yet the final details regarding the evolution of music will be provided by God, who has reserved this revelation for Himself. John said the choir of heaven would exceed one hundred million artists who would be accompanied by trumpets, harps, cymbals, and other instruments. It seems improbable that such a choir could perform in one place at the same time. These singers may be distributed throughout God's new world.

It has been an immense privilege to listen to the great choirs of earth. I have been enthralled by amazing singers in many countries. Who could possibly describe the productions to be made by heaven's international artists? The greatest talents of all time will produce the most attractive music ever heard. Even the angelic hosts will be excited when they hear redeemed saints singing, *"worthy is the lamb that was slain."* Throughout eternity many earthly events will be forgotten. The Bible says, "They will not even come into mind." Yet Calvary will be remembered for ever. Maybe one of the songs to be heard in heaven will be:

66

My Lord has garments so wondrous fine,
And myrrh their texture fills;
Its fragrance reached to this heart of mine,
With joy my being thrills.

Out of the ivory palaces,
Into this world of woe;
Only His great eternal love,
Made my Savior go.

In garments glorious He will come,
To open wide the door;
And I shall enter my heavenly home
To dwell for evermore.
Into the ivory palaces,
Out of this world of woe;
Saved by His great eternal love,
I shall one day go.

Henry Barraclough

THE PURSUIT OF HAPPINESS—
OR HOW TO BE BLESSED BY GOD

Blessed is the man that . . . (Ps. 1:1).

The desire for happiness is shared by every person on earth, but unfortunately the coveted treasure is often elusive. When it appears to be within reach, it slips away, leaving the seeker disappointed and frustrated. Athletes desire fame, politicians seek recognition, misers crave money, but all these things are temporal. Sometimes what takes years to acquire disappears in moments. One of Hollywood's famous film producers who was also a multimillionaire said, "There have been occasions when I would have given everything I possess just for a moment of happiness." Whether it be called serenity, joy, satisfaction, or by any other name, it surpasses all else.

When William Carey went as a missionary to India, he had great dreams for the future of his work. Confronted by many problems he ultimately translated the New Testament into the Hindi language and printed 100 copies, one of which was presented to Queen Victoria. As the years passed, problems increased. Fire destroyed his property, friends failed him, and there were times when he became very discouraged. Then one day, an Indian arrived at the mission bringing a copy of Carey's New Testament. He asked if the missionary had written the book and, receiving an affirmative reply, explained he had been sent by the head of his village. He told how the book had reached his community where one man was able to read. The entire population listened day after day, and strange things began to happen. Drunkenness, immorality, fights, and other forms of vice began to disappear, and the life style of the people changed. The chief wanted to thank the writer of the "little book." The Indian explained he had traveled great distances and visited many places before he met someone able to direct him to the mission. Carey's soul was thrilled.

He had achieved something worthwhile, pleased his Lord, and brought happiness to many Indians. Truly, "the people that walked in darkness have seen a great light: they that dwell in the land of the shadow of death, upon them hath the light shone" (see Isa. 9:2). "Blessed is the man" may be found in many places. There are six Scriptures which, when considered together, provide an exciting sequence of thought.

Blessed Is the Man Who Is Careful

> Blessed is the man that walketh not in the counsel of the ungodly, nor standeth in the way of sinners, nor sitteth in the seat of the scornful (Ps. 1:1).

Life is a highway leading through time toward eternity, and many kinds of travelers can be met thereon. Some may be excellent companions; others are dangerous and should be avoided. It is interesting that in the first psalm David mentions: (1) Walking, (2) Standing, (3) Sitting. Ungodly people are unnecessary companions for pilgrims on their way to the Celestial City. The king knew the results of being influenced by ungodly people. The statement "*the counsel of the ungodly*" suggests someone expressing his views and offering advice. Then suddenly the listener decides to halt. He appears to say, "Stop! That is interesting. Let's have a conference." The travelers were becoming friends. Any person who permits this to happen eventually sits in the seat of the scornful. The man who was a pilgrim going somewhere became motionless going nowhere. David had made this mistake, and in this psalm urged his readers to avoid the pitfalls into which he had fallen. Blessed is the person who is careful. It is better to walk with God than to fraternize with heathens!

Blessed Is the Man Who Considers

> Blessed is the man that trusteth in the Lord and whose hope the Lord is. For he shall be as a tree planted by the waters, and that spreadeth out her roots by the river, and shall not see when heat cometh, but her leaf shall be green; and shall not be careful in the year of drought, neither shall cease from yielding fruit (Jer. 17:7–8).

Undoubtedly, Jeremiah knew David had expressed a similar

truth. The king stressed its negative side, the prophet the positive. Both men made reference to a tree planted by the river. Jeremiah described its phenomenal success amid deplorable conditions. Explaining why the tree produced luxurious fruit, the prophet wrote: "She spreadeth out her roots by the river."

When I was a boy in Wales, grapes were always expensive, for the inclemency of the weather made their cultivation impossible. Sometimes in the south of England a few varieties could be found, but even these had to be grown in greenhouses. Then came the year when everyone became interested in what happened at Hampton Court just outside of London. The royal husbandmen had struggled in vain to grow grapes for the king, but the famous vine never responded. Then, unexpectedly, large bunches of fruit began to form, and the harvest was amazing. When the head man was asked for an explanation, he merely said, "The roots of the vine reached the river Thames." Had Jeremiah been present, he would have smiled and remembered his words, "She spreadeth out her roots by the river."

Isaiah expressed a similar thought when he predicted the future of the people of Judah. He said: "And the remnant that is escaped of the house of Judah shall *again take root downward, and bear fruit upward*" (Isa. 37:31). There is a river which proceeds from the throne of God, and spiritual people draw from its infinite resources. Trees with shallow roots are destroyed by hurricanes; they have no foundations upon which to depend. The same fate threatens people whose roots are close to the surface. *Blessed* is the person who considers these things.

Blessed Is the Man Who Is Chosen

Blessed is the man whom thou choosest, and causest to approach unto thee, that he may dwell in thy courts (Ps. 65:4).

It was never easy to enter the presence of royalty. Few people are afforded that honor. Heads of state and other important officials are frequently given that privilege, but unless some significant deed has been performed, ordinary citizens only see celebrities from a distance. There were some exceptions to the rule. Mephibosheth was permitted to sit at the king's table (2 Sam. 9:11), and the elderly statesman, Barzillai, was offered the same honor. The old man declined the invitation, preferring to remain in his own village (2 Sam. 19:33–35). It is interesting to know the king who gave this honor desired the same for himself in a greater court. He said: "One thing have I desired of the LORD, that will I seek after; that I may dwell in the house of the LORD all the days of my life, to behold the beauty of the LORD, and to inquire in his temple" (Ps. 27:4). It is difficult to separate the reward from the worthiness preceding it. To be *chosen* by the Lord to sit at His table is a reward of incalculable worth. What people are to be *there*, will reflect what they were *here*. "THOU ART WORTHY" is a verdict all would like to hear, but "Many are called, few are chosen." The *blessed* man tries to emulate his Lord, of whom it was written: "Behold my servant, whom I have chosen; my beloved, in whom my soul is well pleased: I will put my spirit upon him, and he shall shew judgment to the Gentiles" (Matt. 12:18).

Blessed Is the Man Who Is Chastised

Blessed is the man whom thou chastenest, O LORD, and teachest him out of thy law (Ps. 94:12).

David and the writer to the Hebrews would have had much in common. Had they lived together on earth they might have talked forever! The king of Israel was said to be a man after God's heart, but he was always in trouble. During the final part of his life his dominant nature asserted itself, and he did things which afterward were regretted. Yet the Lord never forsook His erring child, and ultimately, the contrite monarch was able to write: "Blessed is the man whom thou chastenest, O LORD." Many years later a letter was sent to the Hebrews who were undergoing great suffering. They were reminded that problems are usually followed by peace and praise. The writer said, "Nevertheless *afterward* it [the difficulties] yieldest the peaceable fruit of righteousness" (Heb. 12:11). People with poor eyesight cannot see long distances, and therefore are not interested in the word *afterward*. They want immediate action, and that is not always possible.

The prophet was told to visit the potter's house and learn from what he saw. Enthralled, he watched as a marred and useless vessel was transformed into a thing of beauty. The procedure might have been summarized under four headings (see Jer. 18:1–6):

1. Condemned . . . The vessel was marred.
2. Crushed . . . It was broken so that hindrances could be removed.
3. Controlled . . . The potter made it again.
4. Converted . . . Its uselessness was turned to magnificence.

Wise people are not dismayed by a tempest; they look beyond to the *afterward* and plan what may be done when the sun shines again.

Blessed Is the Man Who Continues

Blessed is the man that endureth temptation: for when he is tried, he shall receive the crown of life, which the Lord hath promised to them that love him (James 1:12).

This text and the promise it contains complement the verses already quoted. A tree that draws nourishment from the river of life does not wither in a drought. The continuous supply of water guarantees its leaves will not wither, nor its fruit be undeveloped. The apostle James lived in an age when many Christians were becoming discouraged. Beset with problems and threatened by death, some were having second thoughts about the advisability of following the Savior. James was a practical man who emphasized that unless faith were supported by deeds, something was wrong with the believer. He wrote about surviving, overcoming, and enduring, and urged his readers to be victorious over their problems. Furthermore, he stated that sufferings experienced in this world were not worthy to be compared with the glory to be known in the kingdom of the Savior. It was significant that when the Lord sent special messages to the churches in Asia, He spoke about rewards to be won through overcoming.

People who accomplished this would experience a closer fellowship with the Lord and in the presence of the angels receive special awards for valor.

Blessed Is the Man That Contemplates

Blessed is the man that heareth me, watching daily at my gates, waiting at the posts of my doors (Prov. 8:34).

Solomon's word picture depicts a man patiently awaiting the arrival of his monarch. Perhaps he was a beggar who had been the recipient of earlier generosity or a friend waiting to greet his lord. *He was willing, waiting, and watching.* He had heard the king was approaching and, with great determination, found vantage point near the palace doors and began his vigil. The royal smile of approval would more than compensate for the time spent waiting. Perhaps the Savior desired to teach a similar truth when He spoke about the maidens who went to meet the bridegroom. At first there were ten, but five were absent when the festivities commenced. The writer to the Hebrews said to his readers: "So Christ was once offered to bear the sins of many; and *unto them that look for him* shall he appear the second time without sin unto salvation" (Heb. 9:28).

Inactivity is not an attribute of the Christian faith. A believer can be exceedingly busy doing the Lord's work and at the same time be awaiting a special sunrise. God said: "But unto you that fear my name shall the Sun of righteousness arise with healing in his wings" (Mal. 4:2). A rising sun heralds the approach of a new day. Blessed is the man who believes the King is coming soon.

The voice of the LORD breaketh the cedars; yea, the LORD breaketh the cedars of Lebanon (Ps. 29:5).

A bruised reed shall he not break (Isa. 42:3).

The twenty-ninth psalm is one of the most descriptive poems of David. He described a tempest felling the cedar trees of Lebanon and spoke of thunder that reverberated through the hills. Bishop Perown says in the *Pulpit Commentary*: "We seem to hear the roll of the ocean, listen to the pealing thunder, to weigh the flash of the lightning, the crashing of trees in the forest, and the heave of the mountains as they were lifted from their foundations by an earthquake. But while it is to the description of all this grandeur and majesty that some commentators chiefly call attention, neither nature's grandeur nor majesty is the main topic of this psalm . . . in the eyes of the psalmist all the forces of nature were under one scepter, wielded by one hand, and that hand was moved by the heart of our redeeming God."

The cedars of Lebanon were among the greatest assets of the country during the reign of David and Solomon. They supplied timber for the temple, and it was valued above many other commodities. Dr. W. M. Thompson says: "I counted 443 trees, great and small. Some are struck down by lightning; broken by enormous loads of snow, or torn to fragments by tempest. Even the sacrilegious axe is sometimes raised against them."[1]

When tempests roared through the mountains, many of these monarchs of the forest were damaged or destroyed. It is possible that at some time or another David witnessed such devastation. The trees which were so tall and stately seemed to brush the stars. When the giants fell, it seemed God's voice had terminated their existence. It was not a cause for amazement when the nation believed thunder to be the voice of the Almighty. James Lee said: "The cedars of Lebanon have always been famous, for they supplied wood for the temple.

One who has visited the forest writes: 'As we stand beneath the great arms of these old patriarchs of a hundred generations, there comes a solemn hush upon the soul as if by enchantment. The girth of the largest tree is more than 41 feet, and the highest may be 100 feet. Some of these are said to be 3,500 years old, but they are not all erect. As we consider these trees, some facts invite attention.

The Majestic Power of God . . . *Great*

> The voice of the LORD is powerful; the voice of the LORD is full of majesty. The voice of the LORD breaketh the cedars; yea, the LORD breaketh the cedars of Lebanon (Ps. 29:4–5).

From time immemorial men considered thunder to be the voice of the Almighty expressing His anger. Modern science has other ways of describing atmospheric disturbances, but even Job said: "God thundereth marvellously with his voice; great things doeth he, which we cannot comprehend" (see Job 37:1–5). Historical events also appeared to endorse that opinion. When the ark of the covenant was returned to Israel by the Philistines, a great assembly of Hebrews gathered at Mizpeh where Samuel interceded for the nation. News of that gathering disturbed the lords of the Philistines who came with a great army to attack the Jews. The Philistines were dismayed and scattered by a terrible thunderstorm which some writers called "God's heavy artillery" (see 1 Sam. 7:10). It became evident that when the Lord spoke from heaven, men were helpless and terrified.

Throughout history, arrogant men imposed their will upon others, and humanity suffered extreme atrocities. The Caesars, Joseph Stalin, Adolf Hitler, and others defied God and sought to take His place. They were foolish men who were destroyed by their ego. It may become possible for other rulers to emulate their example, but the Bible says: "Blessed be the LORD God of Israel from everlasting, and to everlasting" (see Ps. 41:13). Belshazzar, the king of Babylon, was informed by Daniel that his breath was in the hand of God, and that his existence depended upon the mercy of the Lord (see Dan. 5:22–23).

I was at Myrtle Beach in South Carolina just after the terrific storm called Hugo roared in from the Atlantic Ocean. What I witnessed was astonishing. Although many trees were felled by the storm, many were literally twisted as if gigantic hands had endeavored to turn them into corkscrews. Men with their inventions are capable of doing many things but when compared with the forces liberated by God, they are feeble. David had similar thoughts when he wrote: "He breaketh the cedars of Lebanon." When he saw the trees swaying, he compared them with the graceful movements of deer. He wrote: "He maketh them also to skip life a calf" (Ps. 29:6).

The Merciful Pity of God . . . *Gracious*

A bruised reed shall he not break, and the smoking flax shall he not quench (Isa. 42:3; Matt. 12:20).

It was significant that when the dispute arose regarding the legality of healing on the Sabbath day, the Lord withdrew into the wilderness and quoted words spoken centuries earlier by the prophet Isaiah. He used two word pictures which revealed His attitude toward distressed people and spoke of a bruised reed and a smoking flax.

"The pens with which scribes wrote were reeds sharpened at one end. This was dipped into the writing fluid, and messages written on parchment or tablets of clay. It was to be expected that continual use would soften the fibrous point, and when the pen became saturated it would bend and be unfit for further service. The scribe would then crush the softened reed with his fingers and throw it into a container—a waste paper basket! 'Smoking flax [a dimly-burning wick] shall he not quench.' The lamps used in the time of our Lord were made of clay. They resembled a large dessert spoon with a handle at one end and a hole for the wick at the other. The wick, a piece of string, lay flat on the surface of the very small amount of oil within the lamp. Sometimes when the oil supplies were exhausted, the wick slowly burned until only a pinpoint of light remained. Then an offensive odor would be emitted, and an impatient writer instantly extinguished the

76

light by squeezing the wick between his thumb and finger. The prophet said the coming One would be possessed with extreme patience. He would not discard men because they were broken and unreliable, and would not extinguish a light because it had grown dim. The Messiah would replenish the oil, and restore backslidden souls to their former usefulness. The coming King would deliver men, not destroy them."[2]

It is important to remember the same God who broke the cedars of Lebanon looked with infinite pity on a broken reed. The same Lord who felled the trees and made them skip like deer restored people who had become tired and despondent. This was among the greatest of all revelations. God was thought to be austere, but those who knew Him best understood He was filled with compassion. The Lord who brought the universe into existence could charm young children as He held them in His arms. Christians love to sing: "A mighty fortress is our God," but young people sing: "Jesus loves me, this I know, for the Bible tells me so." Would it be correct to describe these extremes as the changing face of God?

The Manifested Pleasure of God . . . *Great*

> The LORD sitteth upon the flood; yea, the LORD sitteth King for ever. The LORD will give strength unto his people (Ps. 29:10–11).

David had already spoken of God's power. Trees were felled, the earth shook, and all nature responded to Jehovah's authority. The psalmist emphasized that God remained undisturbed upon His throne. His ability was unchallenged. He is "from everlasting to everlasting," and no man can change that fact. David proceeded to supply a more intimate glimpse of his Lord. He who broke the cedars of Lebanon and shook mountains was interested in assisting people. He was not a mystical deity living in space but a Father seeking for opportunities to help His children. The psalmist said: "We are his people, and the sheep of his pasture" (Ps. 100:3). A dedicated shepherd loves, listens, and leads his flock. He understands every movement and need of his sheep. He knows when danger threatens and hurries to protect his animals. As David risked his life to defend his flock against the lion and the bear, so the Lord cared for His sheep and was willing to lay down His life on their behalf. The shepherd went ahead of the flock to lead them into green pastures and still waters. At first it appears to be inconceivable that the Almighty who broke the cedars could be kind to suffering people. David was constantly reminded of the protecting power of God who had helped him throughout his life. Nevertheless, it appeared incomprehensible that the Creator of heaven and earth should be anxious to share His life with sinners. The psalmist expressed the same amazement when he said: "What is man, that thou art mindful of him? and the son of man, that thou visitest him?" (Ps. 8:4).

The story has often been told of the child who stood outside the gate of Buckingham Palace. A prince asked what caused his tears, and the boy explained that he wanted to see the queen, but the guard had refused to let him go through the gate. Somewhat amused, the prince took the small boy into Her Majesty's presence and explained the situation. Queen Victoria was a very gracious lady and ordered the child to be bathed and given a new suit before he returned to his home. How could the queen who ruled over a vast empire become the benefactor of a dirty little boy from the street? She had been inspired by the Prince of Peace at whose feet she worshiped.

The Mighty Purpose of God . . . *Glorious*

The LORD will bless his people with peace (Ps. 29:11).

Throughout the long history of the Hebrew nation peace was always elusive. Surrounded by aggressive neighbors, the children of Israel were in constant danger and, apart from the reigns of David and Solomon, were threatened by invasion. The inexcusable persecution perpetrated by Nazi Germany cannot be erased from memory. Yet even in the most distressing periods of their history, the victims believed God would eventually bring them to the time when the lion and the lamb would live peacefully together. That faith has never wavered, and even today there are rabbis who believe their Messiah will make that possible.

It was significant that Jesus said: "Think not that I am come to send peace on earth: I came not to send peace, but a sword" (see Matt. 10:34). It became evident to the disciples that Jesus sought a kingdom within human hearts and not a geographical conquest to expel Romans from the Promised Land. Nevertheless, the Lord also promised to return as the King of Kings and Lord of Lords. His people would indeed be "blessed with peace." This has always been the purpose of the Almighty. John described a city descending from heaven to become the center of righteousness. "And there shall be no night there; and they need no candle, neither light of the sun; for the Lord God giveth them light: and they shall reign for ever and ever" (Rev. 22:5).

The leaders of the early church accepted this fact, and went out to help Christ prepare sinners to become citizens of that amazing city. Without the Gospel, the new Jerusalem would never be inhabited. Millions of Christians believe the establishing of Christ's kingdom will soon take place; the hope of the church is about to become a reality. Selfish governments will no longer covet their neighbor's territory, and armies will no longer dominate weaker nations. Universal peace will continue forever.

> God is working His purpose out
> As year succeeds to year.
> God is working His purpose out,
> And the time is drawing near.
>
> Nearer and nearer draws the time,
> The time that shall surely be;
> When the earth shall be filled
> With the Glory of God
> As the waters cover the sea.

1. W. M. Thompson, *The Land and the Book* (London: Thomas Nelson and Sons, 1910).

2. Ivor Powell, *Matthew's Majestic Gospel* (Grand Rapids: Kregel Publications, 1986).

Blessed is the man whose strength is in thee [God] . . . *who passing through the valley of Baca, make it a well (Ps. 84:5–6).*

The author of this psalm is shrouded in mystery. Some theologians believe the poem was written during the reign of Hezekiah, but there is no conclusive evidence to support that theory. The matter is unimportant, for the writer, whoever he might have been, had discovered a great truth. The text may be divided into three parts. (1) *The Secret*—"The man whose strength is in God"; (2) *The Suffering*—"who passing through the valley of Baca"; and (3) *The Surprise*—"make a well."

The experience described here was probably based on the fact that after being rebuked by God, the Children of Israel shed tears of remorse. The historian wrote: "And they called the name of that place, *Baca*, which meant, *The place of weeping*" (Judg. 2:4–5). It was also called Bochim, but it is difficult to decide its exact location. The name was absorbed into the Hebrew language and became an everyday saying. All kinds of trouble became associated with the Valley of Baca, which also referred to mulberry trees which grew in sandy locations where water was hard to find. The commentator Renan says: "This was the last stage of the pilgrimage from Northern Palestine to Jerusalem. *Ain el-Haramija* is a gloomy, narrow valley where brackish water trickles out of the rocks, and hence, the name *Valley of oozing water* or *valley of tears.*"

When speaking of this text, Andrew Bonar said: "Israelites going to the Passover made light of the deficient water, for their hearts were set on reaching Jerusalem." Those ancient travelers would have appreciated the words spoken by Paul: "For I reckon that the sufferings of this present time are not worthy to be compared with the glory which shall be revealed in us" (Rom. 8:18). The people who journeyed from the north were going to their holy city, and although the sky was ominous, the clouds had silver linings. Even the inhospitable terrain could not discourage the pilgrims, for they thought only of what lay ahead. Problems became avenues of blessing when the vale of tears seemed to be transformed into sparkling water.

Other folk might have considered a similar problem and grumbled. The writer of this psalm had already said: "How amiable are thy tabernacles, O LORD of hosts! My soul longeth, yea, even fainteth for the courts of the LORD: my heart and my flesh crieth out for the living God. Yea, the sparrow hath found an house, and the swallow a nest for herself, where she may lay her young, even thine altars, O LORD of hosts, my King, and my God" (Ps. 84:1–3). Ardent desire will always intensify a man's efforts to reach a goal. This fact is evident throughout the Scriptures.

The Valley Of Difficulty . . . *How Depressing*

Job was probably the first man who could have appreciated the saying: "It never rains but what it pours!" There was a day when four messengers of doom shattered whatever happiness he possessed. Each servant informed his master of a terrible calamity which had destroyed his possessions. The first informed him of an attack made by the Sabeans who had stolen Job's oxen and killed their attendants. The second man described the terrifying fire which had fallen from heaven to destroy the sheep and the shepherds. The third spoke of a raid made by Chaldeans, who had driven away the camels and killed the servants. Finally, the fourth came to relate how Job's children were celebrating in the home of the eldest brother when a hurricane shattered the house and killed his sons and daughters. It may be significant that the survivors did not arrive simultaneously. While one man was making his report the next arrived, until all those frightened men had told their story. Job might easily have said: "It never rains but what it pours."

Then Job arose, and rent his mantle, and shaved his head, and fell down upon the ground, and worshiped. And said, Naked came I out of my mother's womb, and naked shall I return thither: The LORD gave, and the LORD hath taken away; blessed

81

be the name of the LORD. In all this Job sinned not, nor charged God foolishly (Job 1:20–22).

That suffering saint was not aware of the conflict being waged against him by Satan, but he was determined that as he passed through his own personal valley of Baca, he would not dishonor God. The book bearing his name describes the many questions that harassed his mind and the disturbing statements made by friends, but throughout the entire ordeal Job remained unsullied and unshaken. He could have complained that God was unfair, that He had forsaken His servant, but this delightful believer refused to grumble about his circumstances. He transformed his own personal valley of Baca into a refreshing well from which he drew living water. His statement "Though he slay me, yet will I trust him," remains one of the brightest stars in a very dark sky.

The Valley Of Danger . . . *How Deadly*

And David said unto Saul, Thy servant kept his father's sheep, and there came a lion, and a bear, and took a lamb out of the flock: And I went out after him, and smote him, and delivered it out of his mouth: and when he arose against me, I caught him by his beard, and smote him, and slew him. Thy servant slew both the lion and the bear: and this uncircumcised Philistine shall be as one of them, seeing he hath defied the armies of the living God (1 Sam. 17:34–36).

It seems remarkable that when David was confronted by his greatest challenge, he remained serene and undisturbed. He was a youth who led his father's sheep in the fields of Bethlehem and was accustomed to being without human companionship. He possibly charmed angels when he played his flute and perfected his aim when he practiced with his slingshot. He could not have known that his diligence would return amazing dividends. The stone which would be aimed at the gigantic Philistine had to hit its target; there was no room for failure. Goliath was annoyed, insulted, and ready to demolish his youthful antagonist. He had waited for an opponent to come from the camp of the enemy, and the best they could provide was an arrogant child!

Day after day his thundering challenge was heard, but fear had paralyzed the Israelites. They were ready to surrender when David arrived; he was entering a valley of terror. Everybody was petrified except the lad with the ruddy complexion. When he was given permission to confront the giant, he chose pebbles from a mountain stream, and rolling them in his hands, decided they would be suitable for the approaching task. Then he went to meet the giant who seemed as tall as the trees. When Saul and his captains were trembling, David was entering his valley of Baca. He was unafraid, for he considered Goliath to be a dwarf standing in the presence of the eternal God.

> Then said David to the Philistine, Thou comest to me with a sword, and with a spear, and with a shield: but I come to thee in the name of the LORD of hosts, the God of the armies of Israel, whom thou hast defied. This day will the LORD deliver thee into mine hand; and I will smite thee, and take thine head from thee; and I will give the carcasses of the hosts of the Philistines this day unto the fowls of the air, and to the wild beasts of the earth; that all the earth may know that there is a God in Israel (1 Sam. 17:45–46).

It was all over; the giant was dead. David had no problem with his sling, but the sword was heavy. He looked at it and with a great effort completed his task. Then, grabbing the severed head by its hair, he held it high to give encouragement to his astounded countrymen. They had witnessed something which would never be forgotten. The boy had turned a valley of shame into a monument of glory. Unfortunately, later in his life, David was challenged by other giants and was not always victorious. Nevertheless, the splendor of that shining hour would never fade. The shepherd boy had discovered a way by which to transform difficulty into delight. His valley of Baca had become a well from which he drew continuing refreshment.

That ancient story can be as modern as today. Many people face giants of one sort or another, and the prospect is often terrifying. Friends and family frequently fail to understand the predicament when one's outlook becomes threatening. It is never pleasant to walk through the gloomy valley of Baca, where water has a brackish taste, the view of the sky is restricted, and prayers apparently are unheard. Then days seem to be endless, and progress painfully, slowly. David experienced such grief and probably could be an excellent counselor. He asked, "Why art thou cast down, O my soul? and why art thou disquieted in me?" He answered his own question, saying, "Hope thou in God: for I shall yet praise him for the help of his countenance" (Ps. 42:5).

The Valley Of Death . . . *How Demanding*

And they stoned Stephen, [who was] calling upon God, and saying, Lord Jesus, receive my spirit. And he kneeled down, and cried with a loud voice, Lord lay not this sin to their charge. And when he had said this, he fell asleep (Acts 7:59–60).

It is natural for men and women to desire longevity, and unless overwhelmed by pain or devastated by shame, no person wishes to die. Mental illness may upset human reasoning, but it is to be expected that healthy people want to live. Death has always been man's greatest enemy, and every year enormous amounts of money are spent on research, the building of medical facilities, and the training of doctors. Death may come by age, accident, or disease and cannot be permanently prevented. The Bible reveals how certain people endured in their valley of Baca. Luke, the beloved physician of the early church, described the death of the first Christian martyr. Stephen was probably a young man who had no wish to die. He was a convert of promise who assisted the apostles in administering to widows within the church. His great knowledge of the Scripture inspired the sermon delivered to those who sought his death. It appears that his graciousness surpassed his knowledge, for when he was asked to leave his preaching for a less glamorous task, he did not complain. Whether he served in a kitchen or a pulpit, anywhere with Jesus was heaven! This young Christian was the most promising of all the converts and probably that fact disturbed the persecutors who believed their future was being threatened. Stephen was completely fearless when he said:

Ye stiffnecked and uncircumcised in heart and ears, ye do always resist the Holy Ghost: as your fathers did, so do ye. Which of the prophets have not your fathers persecuted? and they have slain them which shewed before of the coming of the Just One; of whom ye have been now the betrayers and murderers (Acts 7:51–52).

The accusations made by the young preacher aroused the anger of his audience who "cast him out of the city, and stoned him: and the witnesses laid down their clothes at a young man's feet, whose name was Saul. And they stoned Stephen [who was] calling upon God, and saying, Lord Jesus receive my spirit. And he kneeled down and cried with a loud voice, Lord, lay not this sin to their charge. And when he had said this, he fell asleep" (Acts 7:58–60).

Stephen was passing through his valley of gloom, but he seemed unaware of his plight. He saw the heavens opened and the Savior waiting to welcome His devoted follower. The psalmist was correct when he explained that anyone making a well in a valley of difficulty was a person whose strength was in God. Death was a tunnel leading to a new country. Stephen was about to meet the King of Kings. He did not die; he fell asleep and awakened in a new world. His homegoing was witnessed by another young man who, many years later, wrote: "O death, where is thy sting? O grave, where is thy victory?" (1 Cor. 15:55). There can never be a shortage of living water, when people know how to make a well in their valley of Baca.

THE ONE WHO COULDN'T
PRAISE GOD ENOUGH!

This is a psalm whose author remains unidentified. He might have been the leader of one of David's choirs, but evidently he was a man absorbed in lyrical poetry. He believed that music was an ideal way to return thanks to Jehovah. This particular psalm has five verses, but they include seven milestones on a highway leading to the heart of God. They are important words: *make, serve, come, know, enter, be thankful,* and *bless His name.* These may be called seven stages of graduation from God's Musical Academy.

Make . . . *The Great Appeal*

Make a joyful noise unto the LORD, all ye lands (Ps. 100:1).

A joyful noise may be interpreted as a shout of acclamation or a cheer, but in this setting it refers to music. The writer seemed to be anticipating the time when all nations would unite in praising God. It would be informative if the historical background of this psalm were known. For example, when David returned the ark to Jerusalem he danced ahead of the procession, and the entire population was filled with jubilation. This poem could easily have been the product of that occasion. Only people out of touch with reality would have been critical on such a remarkable day. The citizens whose faith was in God had every reason to be happy, for the friendship of the Almighty could never be replaced. David was correct when he wrote: "Happy is that people, whose God is the LORD" (Ps. 144:15).

Serve . . . *The Great Acknowledgment*

Serve the LORD with gladness (Ps. 100:2).

Service is the child of praise; intense gratitude begets a desire to share with other people. Only hermits are islands in the ocean of humanity. The people who live alone die without mourners. The ancient writer realized that earthly joys are temporal. Experiences that take a long time to arrive, may depart in moments. Unless blessings are shared, they become memories. The most inspiring testimony is useless unless it is heard. To share gladness is to spread the good news, and privileged indeed is the man who can make people happy. Solomon was wise when he said: "Whatsoever thy hand findeth to do, do it with all thy might; for there is no work, nor device, nor knowledge, nor wisdom, in the grave whither thou goest" (Eccl. 9:10). Unless a man exercises his arm, it may become a useless limb attached to his shoulder. Testimonies are the secret of spiritual enthusiasm. Unfortunately, such services have for the most part been discontinued.

Come . . . *The Glad Acceptance*
Come before his presence with singing (Ps. 100:2).

Come is one of the greatest words in the Scriptures. It is difficult to comprehend that the Creator of the universe desires fellowship with human beings. It would be startling if the Queen of England were consumed with a passion to fellowship with hobos, gypsies, or the poorest of her subjects. It is infinitely more difficult to understand why God constantly urges insignificant people "to come unto Him." The psalmist and his readers were already recipients of God's grace. They had "Come unto God," but were being urged to come repeatedly. They were being invited to drink from a river whose supplies were inexhaustible. This text may be divided into three sections. (1) This is *an extended invitation*. People are never limited in their communion with the Lord. This is not one glorious, never to be forgotten experience; it is an invitation to endless friendship. (2) This is *an extraordinary interview* only known by special people. Money could never purchase the privilege, and fame and repute cannot lead to God's presence. Entrance is only gained through Christ, who said, "No man cometh unto the Father but by me" (John 14:6). (3) This leads to *excellent inspiration*. Joy is expressed in music which God appreciates. The song of the redeemed can only be appreciated by people cleansed in the precious blood of Christ.

And they sung a new song, saying, Thou art worthy to take the book, and to open the seals thereof: for thou wast slain, and hast redeemed us to God by thy blood out of every kindred, and tongue, and people, and nation (Rev. 5:9).

Know ... *The Growing Assurance*

Know ye that the LORD, he is God: it is he that hath made us, and not we ourselves; we are his people, and the sheep of his pasture (Ps. 100:3).

This great text speaks of *the Father who lives*, *the family who is loved*, and *the flock which is led*. It is among the greatest revelations ever made of Jehovah. Surrounded by nations that made and worshiped idols, Israel was commanded to have no other gods beside the Lord. He desired His people to be loyal, and this verse reminded them of that obligation.

The Father Who Lives

The hideous idols manufactured by Israel's neighbors were unable to speak, hear, or move. They were inanimate things unable to respond to the simplest prayer. People liked them because they never rebuked evil. Food placed in their shrine was either eaten by priests or stolen by birds. On the other hand, Jehovah could love and sustain His people and be an intricate part of their daily living. He had created the universe, but it was amazing that He had chosen Israel to be His special joy.

The Family Who Is Loved

"*We are his people.*" God had decided to live among the Hebrews, and His house was in the midst of their camp. No other nation enjoyed that favor. When the Lord issued a command, the tribes were expected to follow His directions. They would be led into green pastures and beside still waters. When they refused to obey the Lord, problems increased and the future became ominous. It was difficult for the people to understand this new concept. They had always feared the Almighty who could shake mountains and divide the sea. The idea of sharing His love was strange, mystifying, and sometimes frightening. It was only when Jesus of Nazareth instructed His disciples that the new revelation became a delight.

The Flock Which Is Led

"We are . . . the sheep of his pasture." An interesting story comes from Switzerland where one day a tourist visiting a shepherd's hut in the mountains saw a sheep with a broken leg. She asked how the accident happened, and was surprised to hear the reply, "I did it." He explained that the sheep was very rebellious. When it would not respond, he broke its leg. He said, "I left it alone for a time, but when I went to feed it the sheep tried to bite my hand. After a few days its attitude had changed; it not only accepted food, it licked my hand." He then said, "Let me tell you something. When this sheep is well, as it soon will be, it will be the best in my flock. No animal will hear my voice more quickly, and none will be closer at my side. That animal has been transformed; it learned obedience through suffering."

Enter . . . *The Grand Advance*

Enter into his gates with thanksgiving, and into his courts with praise (Ps. 100:4).

Some years ago a skeptic asked an evangelist, "Do your converts stand?" He was surprised when the preacher replied, "No, they go forward." It would be encouraging if that were always true, but the writer to the Hebrews expressed the heart of the Christian faith when he said: "Let us labour therefore to enter into that rest" (Heb. 4:11). He made numerous appeals of the same type. "Let us enter" (4:11); "Let us hold fast" (4:14); "Let us come boldly" (4:16); "Let us go on" (6:1). The psalmist would have agreed with his brother of a later age for he also said: "Enter into his gates with thanksgiving, and into his courts with praise." His counterpart said: "Having therefore, brethren, boldness *to enter* into the holiest by the blood of Jesus" (Heb. 10:19). Both writers would have agreed that in spite of what had been received, there was much more available. The desire *to enter* must never diminish. True fellowship with God surpasses everything.

Be Thankful ... *The Great Appreciation*
Be thankful unto him (Ps. 100:4).

Ingratitude is a blight on humanity. When people become the recipients of great generosity, the least they can do is return thanks and be appreciative. God, through His servant Jeremiah, said: "Can a maid forget her ornaments, or a bride her attire? yet my people have forgotten me days without number" (Jer. 2:32). That complaint was repeated again and again (see 3:21; 13:25; 18:15; 23:27). Finally the prophet said: "My people hath been lost sheep; their shepherds have caused them to go astray; they have turned them away on the mountains; they have gone from mountain to hill, *they have forgotten their restingplace*" (Jer. 50:6). The history of the Hebrew nations cited many occasions when God lifted their burdens, solved problems, and delivered them from oppression. Yet they quickly forgot their Benefactor. The people sought God when they needed something but seldom returned thanks for His graciousness. It is wise to remember that even God likes to be thanked. Before the Savior returned to heaven, He instituted the Last Supper and said, "Do this in remembrance of me." He wanted to be remembered.

Bless His Name ... *The Glorious Adoration*
Bless his name. For the LORD is good; his mercy is everlasting; and his truth endureth to all generations (Ps. 100:4–5).

Perhaps the eternal ages will be filled with surprises, for what God has prepared for His people has never been revealed. It is known that heaven will be filled with praise. John was very explicit when he wrote: "And they sung a new song . . . and the number of them was ten thousand times ten thousand, and thousands of thousands" (Rev. 5:9–11). It is impossible to imagine a choir of over one hundred million people. There has never been such a gathering of singers, but the text supports the conclusion that God's country will be filled with harmony. The psalmist believed that joy could be known, at least in part, on earth. Within the short span of five verses in the hundredth psalm, the writer mentioned gladness, joy, and thankfulness seven times. He expressed the desire to make a joyful noise immediately, and thereafter to enter into God's fellowship with songs of praise. Happiness is part of the inheritance of the redeemed. If Christians were required to carry a banner on their pilgrimage to the Celestial City, the words upon it would be BLESS HIS NAME. It is impossible to be bitter, critical, argumentative, resentful, and faultfinding when the soul praises the Lord. It is far better to praise than to pout.

In the year that king Uzziah died I saw also the LORD sitting upon a throne, high and lifted up, and his train filled the temple. . . . And one cried unto another, and said, Holy, holy, holy, is the LORD of hosts: the whole earth is full of his glory (Isa. 6:1, 3).

Isaiah, the evangelical prophet of the Old Testament, was one of the most renowned citizens of Israel. He was honored by all the people and mightily blessed by the Almighty. Recognized as the mouthpiece of the Lord, very little was done without his guidance and approval. He lived in a very difficult age. The king who should have ruled the country had been very foolish and as a result had become a leper. A regent governed the nation, but it was hard to decide who was the most influential—the regent, the high priest, or the prophet Isaiah. The final tragedy came when the ailing monarch died.

And Uzziah the king was a leper unto the day of his death, and dwelt in a several house, being a leper; for he was cut off from the house of the LORD: and Jotham his son was over the king's house, judging the people of the land. Now the rest of the acts of Uzziah, first and last, did Isaiah the prophet, the son of Amoz, write. So Uzziah slept with his fathers, and they buried him with his fathers in the field of the burial which belonged to the kings; for they said, He is a leper: and Jotham his son reigned in his stead (2 Chron. 26:21–23).

The prophet said, "In the year that king Uzziah died I saw also the LORD." Some writers believe this should be the introduction to the entire book. Maybe his ministry began in the year of the king's death. Others believe his *effective* service only commenced then; that previously he had been a prophet, but not a *great* one. Which of the two is accurate is not of great importance, for whenever the anointing came, it revealed certain truths which apply to every servant of God. Six fundamental facts serve as rungs on a ladder that elevates preachers from the ordinary to become extraordinary people whom the Lord can use and trust. It might be helpful to see at a glance the six things that transformed the life of this man of God.

1. His Silent Contemplation . . . Discerning . . ."I saw also the Lord"
2. His Serious Conviction . . . Disturbing . . ."Woe is me"
3. His Sincere Confession . . . Declaring . . ."I am a man of unclean lips"
4. His Sufficient Cleansing . . . Delighting . . ."Thine iniquity is taken away"
5. His Splendid Consecration . . . Deciding . . ."Here am I, send me"
6. His Sublime Commission . . . Dispatching . . ."Go and tell this people"

His Silent Contemplation . . . *Discerning*

A personal confrontation with God leads to two revelations: the holiness of God, and the sinfulness of sin. It is impossible to realize the first without recognizing the second. People may die, but God remains; for when human resources diminish, the sufficiency of the Lord remains unchanged. Today governments are complaining about the crime wave that threatens everybody, but few recognize its cause. When men lose their vision of the Lord, increasing evil is sure to follow. The cure for the world's ill is not increasing numbers of policemen patrolling the streets nor new legislation. Mankind needs to return to God and recapture the vision that inspired our forefathers.

When Isaiah saw the Lord, he became aware of his transgressions. It is not possible to boast in the presence of God. Abraham said, "I . . . am but dust and ashes" (Gen. 18:27). Job said, "Behold, I am vile" (Job 40:4). David said, "Behold, I was shapen in iniquity" (Ps. 51:5). Ezra said, "I . . . blush to lift up my face" (Ezra 9:6). Simon Peter said, "I am a sinful man" (Luke 5:8). The nearer a man gets to God, the more aware he becomes of his shortcomings.

His Serious Conviction... *Disturbing*

It is thought provoking that such conviction should overwhelm Isaiah; he was among the most godly people in Israel. Unlike the publican who cried, "God be merciful to me a sinner," Isaiah was noble, sincere, and dedicated. He was a prince among men. Nevertheless, when he saw the majesty of God he trembled and even forgot to worship. He looked at a palace with an elevated throne and a king whose robes were elegant. When angels chanted the chorus, "Holy, holy, holy is the LORD of Hosts," the prophet felt uneasy. The glory of God was like vapor emanating from an eternal source. It spread until the entire world appeared to be filled with its wonder.

Isaiah became confused and uncomfortable. He felt destitute and unworthy. Self esteem ceased to exist. He was upon holy ground. He wanted to hide, but there was no hiding place. He desired to run, but his legs would not move. Perhaps the writer to the Hebrews had similar thoughts when he wrote: "Looking unto Jesus the author and the finisher of our faith" (see Heb. 12:2). Christians who seldom see the face of God become argumentative, irritable, and unhappy. They resemble oranges from which every drop of juice has been extracted. They are flashlights which produce no light; their batteries are dead!

His Sincere Confession... *Declaring*

Then said I, Woe is me! for I am undone; because I am a man of unclean lips, and I dwell in the midst of a people of unclean lips for mine eyes have seen the King, the LORD of hosts (Isa. 6:5).

It is difficult to reconcile this statement with another recorded in Exodus 33:20: "And he [God] said: Thou canst not see my face: for there shall no man see me, and live." Moses was permitted to see the back of the Lord as He passed through the holy mountain. Perhaps Isaiah saw Him only partially or as one looking from a distance. He was aware that God and His throne were the center of the panoramic view he was permitted to see, but they were not looking into each other's eyes. The vision was sufficient to fill the prophet with a deep sense of awe and unworthiness. The glory of God was indescribable. Isaiah believed he was unworthy to behold the King of heaven. This experience is most essential for all who would serve the Lord. The hymnwriter was truly inspired when he wrote:

> Oh, to be nothing, nothing;
> Simply to lie at His feet:
> A broken and emptied vessel
> For the Master's use made meet.
> Emptied that He might fill me,
> As forth to His service I go;
> Broken that so unhindered,
> His life through me might flow.

His Sufficient Cleansing... *Delighting*

The imagery used in this statement was understood by the prophet's contemporaries. The live coal placed upon the lips of Isaiah cannot be literal, for it would have burned the mouth of God's servant. Some writers suggest it was indicative of the Lord's love which removes sin and inspires the recipient to serve the Lord. The details of the vision are not of great importance. The chief lesson taught is that true cleansing can only be obtained from the Lord. Men who boast of their achievements are seldom close to God. Others who believe themselves to be unworthy are always candidates for divine appointments. The Bible speaks of cleansing by water (John 13:14), by the Word of Christ (John 15:3), and by the precious blood of Christ (1 John 1:7). Even the weakest instrument may become mighty when held by the hand of God.

It is interesting to consider the parallel Scripture in the book of Zechariah. Joshua, the high priest of Israel, was destined for prominence, but unfortunately was unacceptable in his present condition. The account is self-explanatory.

Now Joshua was clothed with filthy garments, and stood before the angel. And he answered and spake unto those that

95

stood before him, saying, Take away the filthy garments from him. And unto him he said, Behold, I have caused thine iniquity to pass from thee, and I will clothe thee with change of raiment. And I said, Let them set a fair mitre upon his head, and clothe him with garments. And the angel of the Lord stood by (Zech. 3:3–5).

The pathway to blessedness begins in humility. A man is never as tall as when he kneels before his Maker.

His Splendid Consecration... *Deciding*

Also I heard the voice of the Lord, saying, whom shall I send, and who will go for us? Then said I, Here am I; send me (Isa. 6:8).

When the Lord asked, "Who will go for us?" He expressed one of the greatest themes in Scripture. Gen. 1:26 tells how God said, "Let us make man in *our* image, after *our* likeness." The same truth is expressed in Isaiah 6:8: "Who will go for *us*?" Evangelical Christians believe in the Trinity, where each member of the divine family is involved in the redemption of mankind. The Father planned it, the Son, the Lord Jesus Christ, made it possible, and the Holy Spirit superintended the entire operation. This has continued since the earliest ages and will continue until time will be replaced by eternity. The triune God was concerned with the need of humanity, but someone had to publish that fact. When Isaiah heard of this need, he volunteered to become God's messenger, and made it clear he was ready to do anything. There were no strings attached.

Isaiah was very different from another prophet who was given a similar assignment. Jonah was told to preach to the people of Nineveh, but he refused to obey and fled to Tarshish. There is significance in the injunction: "Whatsoever thy hand findeth to do, *do it with thy might*" (see Eccl. 9:10). To reject advice or any commission given by the Lord is to exhibit folly. Blessed is the soul who never flinches from his duty. "Not I, but Christ" should be the confession of God's people.

Paul set the pattern for his entire ministry when he asked the risen Christ, "What wilt thou have me to do?" (see Acts 9:6). He did what was required of him and never complained about circumstances. At the conclusion of his ministry the apostle was able to say, "I have fought a good fight, I have finished my course, I have kept the faith. Henceforth there is laid up for me a crown of righteousness, which the Lord, the righteous judge, shall give me at that day: and not to me only, but unto all them that love his appearing" (see 2 Tim. 4:7–8). Diplomas are for graduates—not dropouts!

His Sublime Commission . . . *Dispatching*

And he said, Go and tell this people, Hear ye indeed, but understand not, and see ye indeed, but perceive not . . . Then said I, Lord, how long? And he answered, Until the cities be wasted without inhabitant (Isa. 6:9, 11).

Isaiah's message was destined to be heard around the world. The people of his generation were blind and deaf to God's entreaties and ultimately became slaves of the Babylonians. They deserved their fate, for they disregarded the warnings of the Lord and listened to their own soothsayers. What the prophet was told concerning the future of his generation was literally fulfilled, but the world now knows that he spoke to people of all times and countries. He looked down the corridors of time to see millions of people whose need was as great as his own. He described the Redeemer of the world when he wrote:

He is despised and rejected of men; a man of sorrows, and acquainted with grief: and we hid as it were our faces from him; he was despised, and we esteemed him not. Surely he hath borne our griefs, and carried our sorrows: yet we did esteem him stricken, smitten of God and afflicted. But he was wounded for our transgressions, he was bruised for our iniquities: the chastisement of our peace was upon him; and with his stripes we are healed. All we like sheep have gone astray; we have turned every one to his own way; and the LORD hath laid on him the iniquity of us all (Isa. 53:3–6).

97

At the beginning of his ministry Isaiah said, "Come now, and let us reason together, saith the LORD: though your sins be as scarlet, they shall be as white as snow; though they be red like crimson, they shall be as wool" (Isa. 1:18). Toward its end he tells everybody where to meet with God. As my friend John Moore says in his delightful hymn:

Calvary is the place where my burden was lifted,
Calvary is the place where I was set free;
Calvary is the place where my blind eyes were opened,
Jesus, my Saviour, became precious to me.

*I will say to the north, Give up; and to the south, Keep not
back: bring my sons from far, and my daughters from the
ends of the earth (Isa. 43:6).*

Isaiah was the evangelical prophet. His book spoke of law
and grace, and many of his predictions foretold redemption.
Some of his statements were easily recognized, but others,
equally important, were less conspicuous. The Lord said disobedient Israelites would be scattered to the ends of the earth,
but eventually brought back to their own land. Through His
servant He advised nations to cooperate with the divine program. The Lord commanded people in the Northern Hemi-
sphere to release their hold on the children of Israel and the
nations of the south to follow that example. God told them
plainly *"to keep not back my sons and daughters."*

Pharaoh, the king of Egypt, was an example of one who
deliberately opposed the will of God. He promised to liberate
the Hebrews but always, at the last moment, changed his
mind. It is wise to obey God, for people who refuse lose
everything. The Lord's plans are always beneficial, but often
they require human cooperation. Some folk retain what should
be surrendered.

The Man Who Kept Back Nothing... *Thrilling*

And he [God] said, Take now thy son, thine only son, Isaac,
whom thou lovest, and get thee into the land of Moriah; and
offer him there for a burnt-offering upon one of the mountains which I will tell thee of (Gen. 22:2).

The story of Abraham's willingness to sacrifice his only
son Isaac has attracted universal attention. Moslems, Jews,
and Christians have been fascinated by the account of a father
who was ready to plunge a knife into the heart of his son. The
account has challenged thought in every generation. It was
unnatural for a parent to consent to such a deed and strange
that God should require it.

The early experience of the patriarch may be summarized under three headings: His fear, fellowship, and faith. It is impossible to understand the sacrifice of Isaac without being aware of the spiritual growth of his father. During the early periods of human history it was considered a punishment from God when a man had no heir. A woman was blamed for her inability to conceive, but it was not always her fault. When Abraham accepted his wife's suggestion to permit a maid to bear his child, it seemed an easy solution to the domestic problem. This led to the birth of Ishmael, but Abraham created endless trouble. If he had listened more to the Lord and less to his wife, tragedy would have been prevented.

The patriarch became the friend of God (James 2:23) because he walked with the Lord. He enjoyed fellowship with the Almighty, and that promoted spiritual growth when fear was replaced by faith. That was made possible because the man believed the promises of the Almighty. God indicated Isaac's seed would be as the stars in heaven and sand upon the seashore. The thoughtful parent considered that if Isaac died, he would never become a parent, and the fulfillment of God's promise would be impossible. On the other hand, if the boy were killed the Lord would need to raise him from the dead that the promise could be fulfilled. Centuries later the writer to the Hebrews said:

> By faith Abraham, when he was tried, offered up Isaac and he that had received the promises offered up his only begotten son. Of whom it was said, That in Isaac shall thy seed be called: Accounting that God was able to raise him up, even from the dead; from whence also he received him in a figure (Heb. 11:17–19).

The Bible describes how Abraham's faith was strong even when he journeyed to the place of sacrifice. He said to the young men who accompanied him, "Abide ye here with the ass; and *I and the lad will go yonder and worship, and come again to you*" (Gen. 22:5). Abraham saw not the dagger in his hand, but the faithfulness of God. It may be safely asserted that without that confidence the journey to Mount Moriah would have been unpleasant. It would be interesting to know how much the patriarch understood at that time. When Isaac asked about the lamb, his father replied, "My son, God will provide *himself* a lamb for a burnt offering" (Gen. 22:8). Many years later the Savior said, "Your father Abraham rejoiced to see my day; and he saw it, and was glad" (John 8:56). When the ram took Isaac's place on the altar, the relieved father was elated. His boy would live because the offering died. He had held nothing back from the Lord, and because of his loyalty, he received treasure of incalculable worth. Centuries later Christ said:

> Give, and it shall be given unto you; good measure, pressed down, and shaken together, and running over, shall men give into your bosom. For with the same measure that ye mete withal it shall be measured to you again (Luke 6:38).

The Man Who Kept Back Something . . . *Tainted*

> But a certain man named Ananias, with Sapphira his wife, sold a possession. And kept back part of the price, his wife also being privy to it, and brought a certain part, and laid it at the apostles' feet (Acts 5:1–2).

The account of Ananias and Sapphira is one of the most unpleasant stories in the New Testament. It is impossible to read it without feeling a chill in the human spirit. The sunshine of happiness had risen upon the early church, and believers were rejoicing in what had happened. Then a cloud eclipsed the sun. Two people had dropped dead at the feet of Simon Peter, and, as the news spread, joy disappeared. Some people frowned. Others were critical of God's act, and everybody became apprehensive. Christians desired to know why God had permitted this disaster to overwhelm people who had just made a generous gift to the church. The apostles were solemn, but Peter was not responsible for the tragedy.

The formation of the Christian church had produced unprecedented problems. Difficulties which had only been experienced by individuals were widespread, and thousands of believers were unemployed. Most of the early converts had been employed by Jews who were enemies of the Gospel. Many widows who had been supported by their families had been disowned and left penniless. The apostles recognized the urgency of helping hungry sisters and hastily appointed a committee to supervise the distribution of food and money. Yet it had become evident that more help was required. Some thoughtful Christians sold property and donated the proceeds to the church. There was no law regarding this matter but the love of Christ prompted believers to help their brothers and sisters. Barnabas, Paul's first missionary companion, was a noble example of this kind of generosity (see Acts 4:37).

Within a certain home lived a man and wife who sold a piece of property and later discussed what should be done with their money. They wanted to contribute to the church treasury, but what about their future? If an emergency arose, would they be able to pay their debts? It might be wise to keep a little "for a rainy day." What would Peter say if he became aware of their deed? They shrugged their shoulders and decided this would be their secret.

It has often been claimed that history repeats itself, and this was true in the experience of the two conspirators who paid for their dishonesty. When Naaman, the Syrian general, offered to reward Elisha for services rendered, Gehazi, the servant, was shocked by his master's refusal to accept a gift. Secretly, he followed the former leper, told lies, and obtained illegally what the prophet had refused to accept. When he returned to the house, Elisha asked, "Whence comest thou?" (2 Kings 5:25). The unfortunate man discovered it was impossible to deceive his master, and "he went out . . . a leper as white as snow" (2 Kings 5:27).

If Ananias and Sapphira had explained to the apostles their offering was a part of what had been received for the property, their gift would have been graciously received. When they told lies, their dishonesty had to be exposed to prevent others from corrupting the whole assembly.

A similar truth was taught when God refused to permit

Moses to enter the Promised Land. The patriarch only made one mistake, whereas the people who occupied Canaan were far more unworthy. Yet, as Dr. S. D. Gordon suggested, that incident was invaluable to successive generations of Hebrews. Women taught children about the great leader Moses who did so much for the nation. Their eyes shone with excitement when they heard of the man who defied Pharaoh, but finally the mother would say, "But he was not permitted to enter this beautiful land. He displeased Jehovah, and was denied the privilege." Thus did God teach millions of Hebrews the necessity of obedience.

Similar results were obtained through the death of Ananias and his wife, who might have become famous, but they died in shame. Jehovah only asked for a tithe—one tenth, and possibly these offenders gave more than a tenth. They might have given *MOST* of the purchase price, but their dishonesty destroyed the sanctity of a glorious gift to the Savior.

The Man Who Kept Back Everything . . . *Tragic*

Then Jesus beholding him [the rich young ruler], loved him, and said unto him, One thing thou lackest: go thy way, sell whatsoever thou hast, and give to the poor, and thou shalt have treasure in heaven: and come, take up the cross, and follow me. And he was sad at that saying, and went away grieved: for he had great possessions (Mark 10:21–22).

The statement "Jesus loved him," elevated the young ruler to a place of eminence in the Scriptures. The Son of God loved everybody, so it might seem superfluous to suggest this man had a special place in the affection of the Savior. When the sisters of Lazarus sent to Jesus for help, their messenger said: "Lord, behold, he whom thou lovest is sick" (John 11:3). The writer of the fourth Gospel was also identified as "the disciple whom Jesus loved" (John 13:23). It would appear that these three men shared something unique. The rich young ruler was exceptionally wealthy and was admired by all who sought his advice. If they won approval in his court of appeal, they were elated, but also gracious in accepting defeat. A devout Jew, he had strictly obeyed the commandments of Moses and never asked others to do what he would not. His wealth was so great that if immortality had been for sale, he would have purchased enough for his family and friends. He realized some things were not bought and was candid enough to recognize and confess his need. The man was able to prepare for his funeral, but what lay beyond remained a secret. After death he would be a lonely traveler in an unknown country.

Then one day an itinerant Preacher came to his city to speak about eternal life. Jesus not only made special claims concerning the hereafter, He healed the sick and gave sight to the blind. The young man became so excited, "he came running" (see Mark 10:17). The enthusiasm displayed by a ruler was, to say the least, unusual. Listeners were astonished when he cried out, "Master, what shall I do that I might inherit eternal life?" At that moment evidence was forthcoming to prove good works could not supply what sincere people most desire. "And Jesus looked at him and loved him."

When the Savior said, "One thing thou lackest," it became evident the seeker was within a step of God's kingdom. Jesus appeared to say, "Young man, you have but one step to take." "What is it? Master, what must I do to inherit eternal life?"

Then Jesus beholding him loved him, and said unto him, One thing thou lackest; go thy way, sell whatsoever thou hast, and give to the poor, and thou shalt have treasure in heaven: and come, take up the cross, and follow me (Mark 10:21).

The silence that followed was ominous; the questioner stared into space while Jesus awaited a response. Maybe the angels who walked on streets of gold wondered why the man was reluctant to sacrifice what to them seemed baubles. The decision which was made in a few moments had eternal repercussions. The Bible says: "And he was sad at that saying, and went away grieved: for he had great possessions." As far as is known that ruler never returned. "And Jesus looked round about, and saith unto his disciples, How hardly shall they that have riches enter into the kingdom of God" (Mark 10:23).

Casual readers might infer from this story that only poor people can enter the kingdom of God, but that conclusion would be inaccurate. When God tested Abraham, the patriarch was asked to sacrifice his son Isaac, but it was only a *test*. Isaac was more useful alive than dead. The Almighty was providing Abraham with the opportunity of demonstrating who came first in the patriarch's life. Afterward Jehovah said, "Because thou hast done this thing, and hast not withheld thy son, thine only son: That in blessing I will bless thee, and in multiplying I will multiply thy seed as the stars of the heaven, and as the sand which is upon the sea shore" (Gen. 22:16–17). God is a jealous God. He does not appreciate opposition from His children. Men must choose whether to please themselves or allow Christ to become Lord of their lives. The rich young ruler retained the treasures of earth, but forfeited eternal wealth. Job said: "Naked came I out of my mother's womb, and naked shall I return" (Job 1:21). The treasures of earth are like bubbles, which, when a man grasps, disappear, leaving him with a hand full of nothing!

*And one shall say unto him, What are these wounds in thy
hands? Then he shall answer, Those with which I was
wounded in the house of my friends (Zech. 13:6).*

Jennifer, the youngest member of the family, was usually
subdued when she came to the breakfast table, but one morning her eyes were bright with excitement and her face was
radiant. "Mother," she exclaimed. "Last night I dreamed I
was in heaven, and I saw many wonderful people about whom
I learned in Sunday School. An angel introduced me to Joseph, and David, and Peter, and John, and many others." "And
were you introduced to Jesus?" gently asked the mother. "On,
no, there was no need for that. When I saw the smile on His
face, and saw His arms held out to me, I saw the print of the
nails in His hands." Miss Fanny Crosby would have appreciated the girl's comments for she wrote:

> When my life-work is ended,
> And I cross the swelling tide,
> When the bright and glorious morning I shall see;
> I shall know my Redeemer
> When I reach the other side,
> And His smile will be the first to welcome me.
>
> I shall know Him, I shall know Him,
> And redeemed by His side I shall stand,
> I shall know Him, I shall know Him
> By the print of the nails in His hand.

When the prophet Isaiah spoke on behalf of Jehovah, he
said: "For, behold, I create new heavens and a new earth: and
the former shall not be remembered, nor come into mind"
(Isa. 65:17). All Christians would be delighted to know the
mistakes made during their stay on earth will be obliterated
and eternally forgotten. "They shall not hurt nor destroy in all
my holy mountain: for the earth shall be full of the knowledge

of the LORD, as the waters cover the sea" (Isa. 11:9). Nevertheless, the statement made by Isaiah was not all embracing. Some things will be eternal reminders of the matchless grace of God.

The Irreplaceable Scars . . . *Remaining*

Then saith he to Thomas, Reach hither thy finger, and behold my hands; and reach hither thy hand, and thrust it into my side: and be not faithless, but believing. And Thomas answered and said unto him, My Lord and my God (John 20:27–28).

Thomas was despondent; his Master had been crucified, and the world had fallen apart! The other disciples had changed. Sorrow had been replaced by happiness, but their testimony seemed outrageous. How could Jesus be alive when He was dead? The unbelieving disciple was disgusted—and then Jesus arrived. "Thomas, be not faithless but believing." The poor man seemed to be paralyzed for a few moments and then excitedly, he exclaimed, "My Lord and my God!" He saw the nail prints in the outstretched hands of his Master and heard the invitation, "Reach hither thy finger and behold my hands, and reach hither thy hand and thrust it into my side." Jesus awaited a response which was not forthcoming. Thomas had seen and heard all he desired. Nevertheless, the disciples saw something that day which was incomprehensible. They saw scars destined to be visible throughout eternity.

Zechariah described events to take place preceding the coronation of Christ. He said the returning Messiah would stand upon the Mount of Olives and hold out His arms toward the astonished Israelis. "And one shall say unto him, What are these wounds in thine hands? Then he shall answer, Those with which I was wounded in the house of my friends" (Zech. 13:6). It is intriguing to know that after thousands of years, the scars inflicted on Jesus will still be visible in His glorified body.

It is the fervent hope of all Christians that the mistakes made on earth will someday be completely forgotten. The lame will walk, the blind will see, and the deaf will hear. Wheelchairs will never be needed, hospitals never built. It will be impossible to find a doctor's office. Redeemed saints will possess bodies "like unto his glorious body," for the mortal will have put on immortality, and the corruptible will have put on incorruption. There will never be a blemish, except for those in the side and hands of the Savior. The wound prints inflicted by the Romans, will forever remind the redeemed of the price paid for their redemption.

The Irremovable Stain . . . *Revealing*

> And I saw heaven opened, and behold a white horse, and he that sat upon him was called Faithful and True, and in righteousness he doth judge and make war. His eyes were as a flame of fire, and on his head were many crowns; and he had a name written, that no man knew, but he himself. And he was clothed with a vesture dipped in blood: and his name is called The Word of God. And the armies which were in heaven followed him upon white horses, clothed in fine linen, white and clean (Rev. 19:11–14).

It is believed that when John described the return of Christ, his statement was linked with another made centuries earlier by the prophet Isaiah. "I have trodden the winepress alone; and of the people there was none with me: for I will tread them in mine anger, and trample them in my fury; and their blood shall be sprinkled upon my garments, and I will stain all my raiment. For the day of vengeance is in my heart, and the year of my redeemed is come" (Isa. 63:3–4). John described the battle of Armageddon and the Messiah's ascension to the throne of David when He will reign for one thousand years. The slaying of evil people is not a pleasant thing to consider, but many teachers believe the Lord will be covered with the blood of His enemies. So great will be the slaughter, Isaiah's prediction will be literally fulfilled. "I will stain all my garments." This prophecy might have had an earlier fulfillment, but it must be admitted this gruesome interpretation is not convincing. Other theologians compromise by saying the stained garments may refer to the blood of His enemies *and his own blood.*

It is unwise to be dogmatic in interpreting the Scripture, but certain facts should be considered. The final battle of time will terminate, not as a blood bath, but because of radiation. Writing of the same conflict, Zechariah said: "And this shall be the plague wherewith the LORD shall smite all the people that have fought against Jerusalem; Their flesh shall consume away while they stand upon their feet, and their eyes shall consume away in their holes, and their tongue shall consume away in their mouth" (see Zech. 14:12). The prophet also described how the enemies of Christ will attack their comrades, and there will be no further need for divine intervention. The situation described does not resemble a blood bath, but a deadly catastrophe similar to what happened when American airmen dropped the atomic bombs upon the cities in Japan.

It is necessary to consider another important fact. The only garment to be stained by blood will be the vesture worn by the Savior; the clothing worn by His followers remains *spotless*. John said: "And the armies which were in heaven followed him upon white horses, clothed in fine linen, white and clean." If the Lord leads His armies into a terrible battle, how can the garments of the soldiers be unstained when those of their Leader seem to have been "dipped in blood"? Was God reminding everyone that others remain clean because Christ died to make that possible? "These are they which came out of great tribulation, and have washed their robes, and made them white in the blood of the Lamb" (Rev. 7:14).

The Indescribable Singing... *Resounding*

And they sung a new song, . . . and the number of them was ten thousand times ten thousand, and thousands of thousands (Rev. 5:9, 11).

This is an intriguing Scripture and difficult to comprehend. Whether or not the figures are to be accepted literally is debatable. Ten thousand times ten thousand would be one hundred million. To that must be added "thousands of thousands." It is impossible to visualize a choir of those dimensions. Where would they rehearse? Or, if there were a command performance, where would the presentation be made? It is interesting to remember that Daniel made a prediction closely related to the event described by John.

I beheld till the thrones were cast down, and the Ancient of days did sit, whose garment was white as snow, and the hair of his head like the pure wool: his throne was like the fiery flame, and his wheels as burning fire. A fiery stream issued and came forth from before him: thousand thousands ministered unto him, and ten thousand times ten thousand stood before him: the judgment was set, and the books were opened (Dan. 7:9–10).

The words "ten thousand times ten thousand" are not found in the Greek New Testament. The text must be examined with care. Yet some details cannot be questioned. The apostle was referring to an immense company of singers that included angels, the living creatures, the elders, and the church. They stood around the throne of God to pay homage to the Lamb. It is not known what songs of praise may be included in heaven's repertoire, but evidently these singers were reminding everybody of "the Lamb that was slain to redeem us to God by his blood, out of every kindred and tongue and people and nation." John mentioned two songs which may be listed under one title.

And they sing the song of Moses the servant of God, and the song of the Lamb, saying, Great and marvellous are thy works, Lord God Almighty; just and true are thy ways, thou King of saints (Rev. 15:3).

The song of Moses referred to the redemption from Egypt. The song of the Lamb celebrated the death of Christ and the amazing transformation made possible by His sacrifice. Heaven's music will supersede anything heard on earth. It has been my privilege to listen to great choirs, but nothing ever surpassed what I heard in the villages and schools of native

110

Africa. When I first heard a tune being commenced by an individual, and then slowly, the deep bass voices of the men began to supply harmony, I thought it to be a foretaste of heaven.

When the choir sings in the presence of God, my African friends will be there, and so will the representatives of all nations.

People whose earthly voices left much to be desired will thrill the heart of God. What the Savior did to redeem men and women will never be forgotten, and maybe an old chorus from earth might be heard again.

> Lest I forget Gethsemane;
> Lest I forget Thine agony;
> Lest I forget Thy love for me,
> Lead me to Calvary.

The Incomparable Splendor . . . *Reflecting*

> And I saw heaven opened, and behold a white horse; and he that sat upon him was called Faithful and True . . . and he had a name written, that no man knew, but he himself . . . and his name is called The Word of God . . . And he hath on his vesture and on his thigh a name written, KING OF KINGS, AND LORD OF LORDS (Rev. 19:11–16).

When John described the final events of time, he mentioned four names of the Savior.

1. Relating to His Successful Mission . . ."Faithful and True"
2. Relating to His Strange Mystery . . ."A Name Unknown"
3. Relating to His Splendid Message . . ."The Word"
4. Relating to His Supreme Majesty . . ."King of Kings and Lord of Lords"

These names, although not fully understood, reveal every facet of the Lord's ministry. They reach from everlasting to everlasting—from the eternal ages before time until the Savior will live forever with His bride, the church.

111

Faithful And True . . . *His Successful Mission*

The most eloquent testimony to the faithfulness of Christ was found in His own statement: "And he that sent me is with me; the Father hath not left me alone; *for I do always those things that please him*" (John 8:29). God endorsed that claim when He said, "This is my beloved Son, in whom *I am well pleased*" (Matt. 3:17). Throughout His mission to earth the Lord was true to Himself and to the cause He represented.

A Name Unknown . . . *His Strange Mystery*

And he had a name written, that no man knew, but he himself (Rev. 19:12).

It would be unpardonably presumptive to speculate what Christ's new name will be. Nevertheless, its importance cannot be dismissed, for it was mentioned three times. (1) *It was written on a stone* (see Rev. 2:17). "To him that overcometh will I . . . give him a white stone, and in the stone a new name written, which no man knoweth saving he that receiveth it."[1] (2) *It was written on saints.* "I will write upon him my new name" (Rev. 3:12). This was a reward offered to overcoming Christians. (3) *It was given to the Savior.* "And he had a name written, that no man knew, but he himself" (Rev. 19:12). Whatever that name may be, Christ will share it with His redeemed people when they will be with their Lord throughout the ages. Their association with Christ will be another reminder of the price paid for citizenship in heaven.

The Word . . . *His Splendid Message*

For there are three that bear record in heaven, the Father, the Word, and the Holy Ghost: and these three are one (1 John 5:7).

It seems strange that of all the New Testament authors, only John was impressed by Christ's claim to be *The Word.* The apostle wrote his Gospel, three epistles, and the Revelation and mentioned that name in each of the three types of communication. These references may be classified:

112

The Savior who saved from the penalty of sin.
The Supplicator who saves from the power of sin.
The Sovereign who will save from the presence of sin.

Words are a means of communication; they express thought. The message of God was conveyed through the Savior, who was, is, and ever will be, the divine Spokesman. John's references, when considered in sequence, become exceedingly informative. The Word shared in the counsels of the divine family and helped formulate the plan whereby salvation became possible. John wrote: "And the Word was made flesh, and dwelt among us, and we beheld his glory, the glory as of the only begotten of the Father, full of grace and truth" (John 1:14). God thought it necessary to have a special representative on earth who would be capable of performing what needed to be done. The Word therefore decided to become human. "A body hast thou prepared me" (see Heb. 10:5). The eternal Son was cradled in the womb of Mary and thus became "the only *begotten* of the Father." The Gospel explains how He took sin to the Cross and made reconciliation between God and guilty people.

When John wrote his epistles, he provided a unique glimpse of heaven. "For there are three that bear record in heaven, the Father, the Word, and the Holy Ghost: and these three are one" (see 1 John 5:7). The Savior commenced providing salvation when He was upon earth. He continues that work as the High Priest of His people, and the day is approaching when He will be crowned King of Kings and Lord of Lords, and believers will be delivered from the very presence of evil. Sin will be expelled forever.

Without a word, or words, this world would be a strange place. Men would be isolated without speech, sound, or intelligence. Similarly, without Christ, life would be meaningless. John had rare wisdom when he recognized the importance of a great name—*The Word.*

King Of Kings And Lord Of Lords . . . *His Supreme Majesty*

It should be remembered that during the lifetime of the apostle, kings, and lords represented the most important people

113

in the world. They were either absolute potentates or friends of those who were. Therefore, when John mentioned these names of the Savior, he ascribed to the Lord the greatest honor known to mankind. Jesus was the Supreme One whom all people would adore. It is informative to know that Christ received crowns at least three times. (1) He was crowned with thorns (John 19:2), (2) with glory and honor (Heb. 2:9), and (3) will be the recipient of many crowns (Rev. 19:12). Only then will He have completed the task given by His father.

Prophets predicted the Coronation of Christ. Saints preached about it, and when it happens, everybody will praise the Lamb upon His throne. The words of the poet may ring throughout heaven:

> The head that once was crowned with thorns
> Is crowned with glory now;
> A royal diadem adorns
> The mighty Victor's brow.
>
> The highest place that Heaven affords
> Is His by sovereign right;
> The King of Kings, and Lord of Lords,
> He reigns in perfect light.

When John tried to express what had been revealed to him, his soul was stirred, and he said what every Christian would like to repeat: "Even so, come, Lord Jesus" (Rev. 22:20).

> Jesus shall reign where'er the sun
> Doth his successive journeys run;
> His kingdom stretch from shore to shore,
> Till moons shall wax and wane no more.

---

1. See also Ivor Powell, "The Little White Stone" in *Bible Treasures* (Grand Rapids: Kregel Publications, 1953).

SECTION TWO
The New Testament

I indeed baptize you with water unto repentance: but he that cometh after me is mightier than I, whose shoes I am not worthy to bear: he shall baptize you with the Holy Ghost and with fire (Matt. 3:11).

One of the most interesting and challenging things about the inspired servants of God is that during their lifetime something happened to change them. For example, D. L. Moody, the great evangelist, described a time when his ministry was revolutionized. Prior to that experience he was a very ordinary pastor, and unfortunately nothing of great importance ever occurred. Then came the blessed anointing. He said, "I preached the same sermons, but God's blessing rested upon them in a way I had never known." John Wesley, Finney, and a host of great Christians shared a similar experience. Something outstanding changed their lives; they were never the same again. New zeal burned within them, and multitudes of souls were brought into the kingdom of God.

Unfortunately, instead of desiring a similar experience, theologians began debating about its validity, and this brought conflicts to the churches. Some people said it was "a second blessing," but others stated it was a natural development from conversion. They argued that since every Christian is a temple of the Holy Spirit, there was no need for Him to enter the believer the second time, but He could arise from within to anoint believers with fresh power. All kinds of definitions began to appear within the vocabulary of the church. Preachers expounded on the benefit of total surrender, sanctification, the fullness of blessing, and the anointing, etc. Yet it was conspicuous that while these ministers argued about interpretation, they continued to preach to empty pews. They were more eloquent than efficient. They did not explain how Moody had been changed from a mediocre pastor to one of the greatest soul winners.

John the Baptist said he baptized with water, but the Messiah would baptize with the Holy Spirit and with *fire*. Most people are acquainted with immersion in water but remain ignorant of the new baptism to be given by Christ. Fire is associated with action.

Any sportsman who exhibits enthusiasm is said to be fiery, that is, energized by a new wave of emotion. A man of fire is like an athlete who runs like a deer, he shouts like a politician, convinces like a salesman, and waves his arms like a windmill! It should be recognized that this baptism of fire is not excessive shouting from a pulpit, for empty barrels sometimes make the most sound. Some eloquent auctioneers sell junk! History suggests that when Christians are completely dedicated, the Lord, in an unmistakable fashion, anoints them with ability to do what earlier was impossible. The soul will be warmed with the presence of Christ, which makes everything else insignificant.

People ask, "Have you been baptized with the Holy Spirit?" The answer should be sought not in words, but in the service being rendered for the Savior. There are people who claim to have received all kinds of spiritual gifts, but their deeds do not endorse the statements made. They are self-centered, obnoxious, and repulsive. They speak about the fire of the Divine Spirit, but their hearts remain cold. There is no way of knowing what sermon topics occupied the attention of the pastors of the Laodicean church, but they might have spoken about the power of the Holy Spirit when their own souls remained lukewarm (see Rev. 3:14–22).

It should be remembered that John the Baptist did not speak to theological students. He addressed a multitude of people who "went out to him [from] Jerusalem, and all Judaea, and all the region round about Jordan" (Matt. 3:5). Whatever the "Baptism with Fire" was to be, it was meant for everybody and not reserved exclusively for men who were destined to become apostles. Every Christian minister needs it, as do others from all walks of life. We all need it, for this was the gift which enabled the early believers who, when they were persecuted, "went every where preaching the word" (see Acts 8:4).

God's Fire Purifies... *Completely*

But who may abide the day of his coming? and who shall stand when he appeareth? for he is like a refiner's fire, and like fullers' soap. And he shall sit as a refiner and purifier of silver: and he shall purify the sons of Levi, and purge them as

117

gold and silver, that they may offer unto the Lord an offering in righteousness (Mal. 3:2–3).

Matthew described how, after the Lord cleansed the temple, the lame and the blind came to Him in the sanctuary, and He healed them (see Matt. 21:14). This was to be expected. First, the Savior expelled the people who defiled the house of God, and then He filled it with His glory. Malachi predicted this would happen. The Lord could not fill a filthy house with the glory of God, and that fact remains unchanged. When the prophet delivered his message, the refining of gold and silver was a simple process. I have seen the machines used in the gold fields of South Africa, in which the ore is crushed and the precious metal extracted. Malachi was unacquainted with such complicated methods. He only knew of the craftsman who sat with a crucible and carefully controlled the refining fire. It is claimed he knew when the process was complete when the reflection of his face could be seen in the molten metal. The fire of God purifies the most precious things in existence—the immortal souls of the people for whom Christ died. This process is necessary, for without it, entrance into the city of God will be denied. "Nothing that defileth shall enter therein" (Rev. 21:27).

God's Fire Prevails . . . *Consistently*

[Elisha] took up also the mantle of Elijah that fell from him, and went back, and stood by the bank of Jordan; And he took the mantle of Elijah that fell from him, and smote the waters, and said, Where is the LORD God of Elijah? and when he also had smitten the waters, they parted hither and thither: and Elisha went over (2 Kings 2:13).

And suddenly there came a sound from heaven as of a rushing mighty wind, and it filled all the house where they were sitting. And there appeared unto them cloven tongues like as of fire, and it sat upon each of them (Acts 2:2–3).

Then they that gladly received his word were baptized; and the same day there were added unto them about three thousand souls (Acts 2:41).

118

It is significant that before Elisha wore his master's mantle, he destroyed his own garments. They were no longer needed. He had requested a double portion of the prophet's spirit be given to him, and that request was granted. He performed twice as many miracles as did his master. The ancient story provides a prototype of what happened to the disciples after their Master ascended into heaven. What had been a small flame became a raging fire of devotion and enthusiasm which evangelized the world. It is unbelievable that men who had been disappointing and unreliable succeeded in leading thousands of souls to Christ. Evidently something happened both to Elisha and to the disciples of Jesus. They were transformed by the power of the Holy Spirit. Feeble, ineffective men became invincible. That experience should be sought by every Christian. It would replace defeat with victory which the gates of hell could not withstand. Elisha refused to leave his master. He remained with him until the end. Does this have any connection with the fact that, although five hundred people began the prayer meeting which preceded the day of Pentecost, only one hundred twenty endured to the end? So many Christians resemble the believers in Galatia of whom Paul wrote: "Ye did run well; who did hinder you?" (Gal. 5:7).

The disciples who were present when the Holy Spirit came had plenty of time in which to reflect, repent, and renew their vows. They understood, as did Elisha, there was no need to depend upon human resources. They relied entirely upon the Holy Spirit. The Heavenly Refiner was gazing intently at His precious metal and was pleased to see His reflection. Dross had been removed and the disciples made ready to be instruments of the living Christ. If this self-examination had not preceded Pentecost, the outpouring of the Holy Spirit might have been delayed or abandoned. God used people who were completely dependent upon Him. He used clean vessels and not those filled with cobwebs!

Perhaps there is a shortage of such people today because many Christians dislike the heat of God's refining fires. When the revival came to Wales in the year 1904, God's power fell upon a young man named Evan Roberts who was troubled by the complacency of his nation. After attending a service in the church, he knelt in the middle of a field and prayed all night. He was still on his knees at dawn. When he began his vigil, he was an inexperienced Christian. He arose a man of God prepared to lead the greatest crusade ever experienced in his native land. This was his baptism of fire. Apparently, he did not speak in tongues as did the apostles, but he worked overtime using what he already possessed. We all need a similar experience. Beginning with the ministers and continuing to the youngest members of the church—everybody needs to be anointed with the Holy Spirit *and with fire*!

God's Fire Protects . . . *Continually*

Can a man take fire in his bosom, and his clothes not be burned? Can one go upon hot coals, and his feet not be burned? (Prov. 6:27–28).

Solomon was a very observant man. Many of the simple things he saw were expressed in proverbs now known throughout the world. Unfortunately, in spite of the wisdom with which he had been endowed, the king rejected the advice given to others and became a victim of his lust. The unholy fire which he permitted to burn within his soul became an inferno which destroyed him.

We never saw brush fires in Wales, for intermittent rain kept everything damp. Once there was a small outbreak on the mountain, and it created national interest. When I came to California, I learned how people fight fire with fire. Back fires are used to destroy the vegetation ahead of the approaching danger. Things would have been different during the reign of Solomon had the king been acquainted with this procedure. Paul reminded the Philippians of the desirable fruit of the Spirit and then urged them to *"think on these things"* (see Phil. 4:8). When the holy fire of God burns within the Christian's mind, its power destroys everything which is a menace to spirituality.

> Breathe on me, Breath of God
> 'Till I am wholly Thine,
> Until this earthly part of me
> Glows with Thy fire divine.

Come ye yourselves apart into a desert place, and rest a while (Mark 6:31).

It has often been said that eyes are the windows of the soul. It may also be claimed the words of a poet are the highways of his mind. A man may reside in a desolate area, his surroundings may be drab and gray, but his ability to rise above the ordinary suggests an eagle majestically soaring above storms. A true dreamer never encounters travel restrictions. He can climb mountains, explore valleys, be enthralled with a bird skillfully making its nest, or thrilled with lambs playing in a meadow. Without money or passport he can be a world traveler and never leave his home. Probably Jesus of Nazareth appreciated this fact. He loved the hills where the silence was unbroken except for the cry of a bird or the whisper of an angel. When the tension was great in the valley and the Lord and His friends had no time to enjoy a meal (see Matt. 6:31), the Savior went into the wilderness seeking rest and contemplation. Sometimes crowds of thoughtless people thwarted His plans, but as soon as it became possible, the Lord climbed the mountain to sit down with God. That was the secret of His unruffled confidence. He never became irritable nor shouted at an offending disciple. The poet captured that serenity when he wrote:

> O Sabbath rest by Galilee,
> O calm of hills above.
> Where Jesus knelt to share with Thee
> The silence of eternity,
> Interpreted by love.
>
> Drop Thy still dews of quietness
> Till all our strivings cease.
> Take from our lives the strain and stress,
> And let our ordered lives confess
> The beauty of Thy peace.
> Frederick C. Maker (1844–1927)

It should always be remembered that even the best of God's servants are human. The most successful of His laborers may have "feet of clay." If a Christian makes a mistake, he is invariably condemned, when he needs understanding and sympathy. Paul expressed the mind of God when he wrote: "Brethren, if a man be overtaken in a fault, ye which are spiritual, restore such an one in the spirit of meekness; considering thyself, lest thou also be tempted" (Gal. 6:1). A helping hand is better than a fist, a benediction more acceptable than a blow. When extreme tension overwhelms a worker, and the selfishness of critics devastates his soul, retaliation is often forthcoming. Unfortunately a lashing tongue does more damage in moments than can be repaired in months or even years. A walk in the countryside is better than a stay in the hospital or an argument in a court of law. When feelings are hurt and a desire to "get even" is evident, angry people should remember and accept the advice given in the spiritual:

> Steal away; Steal away;
> Steal away to Jesus.
> Steal away, steal away home;
> I ain't got long to stay here.

The Concerned Preachers... *Frustrated*

And the apostles, when they were returned, told him all that they had done. And he took them, and went aside privately into a desert place belonging to the city called Bethsaida (Luke 9:10).

The disciples were becoming apprehensive. Their sky which had been filled with the sunshine of expectation was overcast. The arrival of John's disciples, who described the execution of their master, seemed to be a warning of worse things to come. Herod, who boasted of the demise of one preacher, was now asking, "Who is this Jesus?" The disciples were worried. The news of the brutal killing of the wilderness evangelist filled them with grief. The continuing demands of the huge crowd were beginning to annoy the weary men. Thousands of strangers thought only of themselves and had no consideration for other people. It was impossible to prepare and enjoy a meal without interference. There was a limit to everything. The disciples were overworked, tired, and irritable. Then the Lord suggested a ride in a boat, and the idea was brilliant.

At last there was an opportunity to escape from the people who were causing all the trouble. Their Master understood the situation. The boat was launched, the sail set, and the journey to tranquillity commenced. Some of the men closed their eyes or gazed longingly at the distant hills. It was very relaxing until one of the party growled his disgust. He was watching the crowd running around the northern shore of the lake. The multitude would be awaiting their arrival. Smiles became frowns as the disciples recognized what was taking place. Why couldn't those folk go home? Had they nothing else to do than monopolize the Master's time? Jesus alone remained calm. His eyes reflected the compassion within His heart. He also was exceptionally weary but not too tired to respond to a mother begging healing for her child.

The Lord knew His followers needed rest, and although His immediate plan was ruined, as soon as it became possible He would lead His servants to another resting place. Blessed is the man who can choose between rest for himself and the privilege of helping others. Some unwise Christians, refusing to rest, hurry toward their grave. They not only burn a candle at both ends, they invent means by which to burn it in the middle as well. Everyone needs to be reminded that Satan applauds such foolishness. The Evil One would be willing to send flowers to the funeral of any worker who, refusing to rest, shortens his life. When God gave brains to people, He expected them to be used!

The Criticized Patriarch . . . *Furious*

And it came to pass on the morrow, that Moses said unto the people, Ye have sinned a great sin: and now I will go up unto the LORD; peradventure I shall make an atonement for your sin. And Moses returned unto the LORD, and said, Oh, this people have sinned a great sin, and have made them gods of

gold. Yet now, if thou wilt forgive their sin—and if not, blot
me, I pray thee, out of thy book which thou hast written
(Exod. 32:30–32).

With the exception of the Savior, Moses must be the most
honored Bible character. People speak enthusiastically about
Job, but this leader of Israel exhibited more patience than any
other man. How he succeeded in leading a complaining nation
through inhospitable territory for forty years is beyond
comprehension. He appeared from nowhere, challenged the
most powerful man in the world, demoralized a trained army,
and rescued a nation of slaves. This story has inspired writers
in all ages. Moses strengthened the desire for freedom, and
under his guidance liberation was ultimately obtained. Yet,
the ingratitude of the Hebrews beggared description, for at
every opportunity they rebelled against leadership and accused
Moses of interfering in their lives. Defiantly, they made a
golden calf and danced naked before it. Their attitude was so
disgusting that the patriarch became furious, and for one
outburst of anger, that great man was prevented from entering
Canaan. If he lived on earth today, Moses would be awarded
the greatest honor known to man. When God offered to
abandon Israel and make a new nation with him as its leader,
the patriarch refused the offer and asked God to forgive his
offensive brethren (see Exod. 32:10–11).

It is wise to remember that Moses was not an angel nor
some other supernatural figure—he was a man acquainted
with human weakness. This author has often confessed that
had he been the leader of Israel, those unworthy people would
have reaped the reward of their deeds! How that man remained calm amid such intolerable criticism defies explanation. Perhaps his simple statement, "I will go up unto the
Lord," explains the secret of his success (see Exod. 32:30).
When other leaders like James and John would have called
fire from heaven (see Luke 9:54), Moses climbed the mountain and shared his problems with the Almighty. It is better to
reflect than to rant and rave! When the healing power of
God's grace began to fill the irritated soul of the distressed

leader, peace became a reality. David knew something of this experience, for he wrote: "I will lift up mine eyes unto the hills, from whence cometh my help" (Ps. 121:1).

The Confused Prophet... *Fearful*

> And he [Elijah] came thither unto a cave, and lodged there; and behold, the word of the LORD came to him, and he said unto him, What doest thou here, Elijah?... And it was so, when Elijah heard it, that he wrapped his face in his mantle, and went out, and stood in the entering in of the cave. And behold, there came a voice unto him, and said, What doest thou here Elijah? (1 Kings 19:9, 13).

If Moses may be compared with the moon which shone in a dark sky, Elijah was a shooting star. His coming was unexpected. He left a fiery trail and then disappeared as quickly as he came. Yet he dazzled the people of his generation and earned an abiding place in history. After his sudden, but extraordinary, departure from this world, he was seen again speaking with Christ on the Mount of Transfiguration (see Matt. 17:3). His ministry did not terminate; he will be one of the two witnesses to resist evil in the closing days of time (see Mal. 4:5; Rev. 11:3).

His ministry cannot be forgotten, for he did the impossible. Elijah was truly a man of fire, whose exploits may be summarized thus:

1. His Fiery Denunciation . . . Startling
2. His Fiery Display . . . Spectacular
3. His Fiery Departure . . . Saddening

He closed heaven for three and a half years so that no rain fell. He defied the prophets of Baal and brought a rebellious nation to its knees. He could have been the greatest evangelist of all time, but unfortunately he became scared of a woman, and his faith failed as he fled. After a journey of forty days and forty nights, he found a cave in the mountain and, stumbling into the darkness, believed his ministry had terminated.

125

Then he discovered he had company. At first he was unaware that the Almighty was awaiting the arrival of his despondent servant.

> . . . and, behold, there came a voice unto him, and said, What doest thou here, Elijah? (1 Kings 19:13).

Standing in the mouth of the cave, the prophet saw the destructive power of the tempest as the wind rushed through the canyons, but his eyes remained bleak. When an earthquake rocked the foundation of the mountain, he trembled, but the awesome shaking left his soul unmoved. Then a soft and gentle whisper broke his resistance, and he fell into God's everlasting arms. He had destroyed his reputation as a fearless preacher, but neither he nor any other person could destroy the matchless love of God. A new beginning awaited him, and with fresh resolution gleaming in his eyes, Elijah descended the mountain. This is a lesson Christians need to learn. Every preacher at one time or another believes himself to be a failure. God did not shout at His forlorn servant. *He whispered*, and a dying spirit was rejuvenated. Jehovah is the Great Physician, capable of restoring health to a weary soul. The moral of this ancient story is easily understood:

> Be not dismayed whate'er betide,
> God will take care of you!

WHAT HAPPENED WHEN
CHRIST WENT TO CHURCH!

Originally, there was only one place of worship in Israel. At first it was a tent—the tabernacle which God commanded Moses to erect among the Hebrews as they journeyed from Egypt to the Promised Land. This was followed by a temple which David prepared and Solomon built in Jerusalem. All the national festivals were held there and every family was expected to attend. This custom continued until enemies destroyed the sanctuary and confiscated its treasures. At one time in their history Hebrews were forbidden even to visit the city of their fathers. Subsequently, other arrangements were made, and synagogues began to make their appearance in many Hebrew communities. It was more convenient for Jews to worship in their own locality than to make the long journey to Jerusalem.

These buildings were not used exclusively for religious services. They were educational centers, where rabbis instructed children; social centers; and occasionally, when travelers needed accommodation, the synagogues became hostels. Many activities were held there, but on the Sabbath, God was honored and the laws of Moses explained. The entire life of the community revolved around the sanctuary. It could be compared with the meeting house which stood at the center of every Maori village in New Zealand, or the local chapel such as I knew in the valleys of Wales. Such churches were available for use at any time, and every person in the community respected the house of the Lord.

When Jesus began to preach in Galilee, synagogues had been erected in many of the cities, and it was in them He delivered His first messages. It is a safe assumption that during the Lord's lifetime, most Jews attended the synagogue. It was incumbent upon all citizens to support their local rabbi.

Hebrew services have changed considerably. When I attended the synagogue in Pretoria, South Africa, I was introduced to something I never before experienced. There was a high pulpit at one end of the building, and the congregation of men faced each other across the sanctuary. The singing was led by the Cantor—church people would call him the director of music. When he sang, every person was attentive. He possessed a marvelous voice, and his boys' choir, which occupied seats in the balcony, would have charmed angels. I was astounded when the rabbi delivered his sermon, for many in the congregation began to read newspapers. The women who were seated near the choir did not listen for they were staring at me—the visitor who wore a clerical collar! There is no way of knowing whether such conditions prevailed when Jesus went to the synagogues, but a verse in the Gospels deserves examination.

A Continuing Custom... *Remarkable*

And he came to Nazareth, where he had been brought up: and, as his custom was, he went into the synagogue on the sabbath day, and stood up for to read (Luke 4:16).

The early life of Jesus remains shrouded in mystery. When He was twelve years of age, He accompanied Joseph and Mary to the feast at Jerusalem, but what happened during the following eighteen years is unknown unless it is gleaned from certain texts. Tradition suggests He worked in the carpenter's shop owned by Joseph, and it is believed He lived with His parents. Luke says the Lord attended services in the synagogue every Sabbath. *This was His unchanging custom.* Unless circumstances prevented this, *Jesus was present at every service.* Was He ever bored, disappointed, or angry? Did the rabbi speak for thirty minutes and say nothing? Did the priest express all kinds of ideas but fail to stir the souls of the congregation? Were the eyes of the Savior alight with pleasure, or did His face reflect disappointment as He listened to mere dogma? It is not known whether or not the Lord enjoyed those services, but one fact remains irrefutable—*He continued to attend.* That custom continued throughout His life and should be emulated by every believer.

When Christians refrain from attending church, they become the equivalent of the unfortunate people who sleep on sidewalks and park benches. They are God's homeless people. As Jesus attended the services in the synagogues, certain things became evident.

His Faith

When people saw Jesus worshiping in the synagogue, it became evident He was a devout believer in God. He often climbed the hills to be alone with His Father and probably enjoyed that experience far more than listening to something already known. The Lord knew critics were watching, and if He expected others to attend the house of God, it was necessary to set a good example. When the writer to the Hebrews wrote to his friends he said: "Not forsaking the assembling of ourselves together, as the manner of some is" (Heb. 10:25).

His Fellowship

People need fellowship; hermits seldom help anybody. The Master enjoyed lifting burdens and solving problems, and it was significant that several miracles were performed in synagogues. It is not difficult to visualize the Savior's moving among the congregation and enjoying every contact, especially with children. A sanctuary is an excellent place to meet people. Less attractive persons do not find pleasure in the House of God.

His Finances

The Lord never had any spare money. The financial resources of the disciples were held by Judas, and it is significant that in order to pay His taxes, Jesus sent Peter on a fishing expedition (see Matt. 17:27). It was customary for worshipers to bring an offering to the temple services, and this applied also to synagogues. The Lord who saw a widow placing two mites into the treasury (see Mark 12:42) would obviously bring His gift. Probably it was not great, but its value was multiplied by love. Men who never support God's cause inevitably die poor! God promised to honor those who honored Him, and such a reward could hardly be given to misers. Although it became evident that Jesus did not agree with everything taught by the rabbi, His opinions did not prevent Him from bringing a gift to support God's work. Wise Christians follow His example.

His Feelings

The Son of God came to earth to help people, and these could always be found near the sanctuary. Some came to beg from affluent visitors. Others realized God alone could heal their diseases. Luke described how the Savior restored life to a man's withered arm. Blessed are they who truthfully say, "I went to church and met Christ." Most people attend places of worship in the hope of receiving something. Jesus went to give. It is interesting to remember that although He was always busy, He made a special effort to be in the sanctuary on the Sabbath. It would be refreshing if this could be said of all who claim to be God's children.

A Contemptible Congregation . . . *Rejecting*

The citizens of Nazareth were interested in one of their Sabbath school scholars. Jesus, whom they all knew, had suddenly become famous. His miracles had thrilled the people of Galilee, and His fame had spread throughout the area. Rumor said he was expected to attend the service, and the synagogue was filled when He entered the building. Silence followed the initial excitement, and the audience watched as the priest invited Him to read the lesson chosen for that day. The Lord found the selected place and began to read.

> The Spirit of the Lord God is upon me; because the LORD hath anointed me to preach good tidings unto the meek; he hath sent me to bind up the brokenhearted, to proclaim liberty to the captives, and the opening of the prison to them that are bound. To proclaim the acceptable year of the LORD (Isa. 61:1–2).

Jesus was gracious, appealing, and commendable. "And all bare him witness, and wondered at the gracious words which proceeded out of his mouth" (Luke 4:22). Did the listeners wonder why He stopped so abruptly? The Lord closed the book without saying *"And the vengeance of our God."* When He said, "This day is this scripture fulfilled in your ears," the listeners became restless. The Carpenter was insinuating He was the fulfillment of the Messianic prediction. When they said, "Is not this the son of Joseph?" the Savior's spirit was chilled. They did not understand the day of vengeance had *not* arrived. Christ terminated the reading so suddenly because He was introducing a period of unprecedented blessedness. The congregation expressed their doubt by asking, "Is not this the carpenter's son?"

They continued listening, but then the sanctity of the service was shattered. "All they in the synagogue, when they heard these things, were filled with wrath. And rose up, and thrust him out of the city, and led him unto the brow of the hill whereon the city was built, that they might cast him down headlong. But he passing through the midst of them, went his way" (Luke 4:28–30). Unfortunately, the miracles witnessed in Capernaum were never seen in Nazareth. The citizens knew not the time of their visitation. Christ came to His own, and His own received Him not (see John 1:11).

A Chilling Cry . . . *Resounding*

And [Jesus] came down to Capernaum, a city of Galilee, and taught them on the sabbath days. . . . And in the synagogue there was a man who had a spirit of an unclean devil, and cried out with a loud voice, . . . And Jesus rebuked him, saying, Hold thy peace, and come out of him. And when the devil had thrown him in the midst, he came out of him, and hurt him not (Luke 4:31–36).

I have visited what is left of the ancient synagogue in Capernaum. The long stone bench upon which sat the elders has survived the attacks of weather, fire, and invading armies, but the smoke blackened beams indicate the ferocity with which Roman soldiers ruined the place. Long ago that sanctuary was probably filled with Jewish families that came from the nearby homes, and among the congregation was Simon Peter and members of his family. His wife was at home caring for her sick mother. The day was destined to become memorable, for both the Savior and a devil had come to church! Everything was peaceful and calm until Jesus entered the building, but then a screeching voice shouted, "Let us alone. What have we to do with thee, thou Jesus of Nazareth? Art thou come to destroy us? I know thee who thou art; The Holy One of God" (Luke 4:34).

One wonders what would happen if that scene were repeated today! Women might gasp, elders would attempt to remove the man, and the pastor would wish he were on vacation!

It is thought provoking that demons recognized the Lord while the congregation only saw a visitor. "We know Thee" was a claim Jesus could not deny. If those evil spirits had been expelled from heaven when their leader Lucifer fell from high office, they had not forgotten the glory of the One by whom all things existed (see John 1:1–3). Three details should be considered. (1) *FEAR*. Evidently the demons were scared, for they knew Jesus had the power to destroy them. That will be their fate when everything unclean is banished from God's new world. (2) *FAME*. "And the fame of him went out into every place of the country round about." God's presence had filled His house. The fact that such power is seldom seen today remains a cause for regret. (3) *FELLOWSHIP*. After the service in the synagogue, Jesus was invited to share a meal in Peter's nearby home. When He heard of the illness of Simon's mother-in-law, Christ healed her and smiled as the delightful lady hurried to the kitchen either to prepare or superintend serving the meal. She knew it was better to be on her feet helping than to be on her back doing nothing. It was thrilling when Simon Peter discovered the blessings experienced in the sanctuary could be greater in his own home. As it was then, so it can be today for all who invite Christ to share their hospitality.

*And as he spake, a certain Pharisee besought him to dine
with him; and he went in, and sat down to meat (Luke 11:37).*

Throughout the Middle East it is considered a great honor
to share a meal in the home of an official. If a sheik entertains
people, it is always a very lavish occasion when guests are
treated as royalty. This was evident during the life of the
Savior. Various people for different reasons invited the Lord
into their homes, but sometimes their motives were suspect.
Matthew, the publican, made a feast to introduce friends to
the Lord (see Luke 5:27–29). Martha of Bethany invited Jesus
into her home because she desired to entertain the One who
had captured her admiration (see Luke 10:38). Zacchaeus descended from the branches of a tree to become the host at a
hastily arranged party for the Lord (see Luke 19:5–6). It is
disappointing to discover a Pharisee who asked the Lord to
share a meal, hoping legal friends would be able to discredit
the Savior's teaching. He and his colleagues disliked what
they had heard and planned to refute His statements. When
the Lord entered that home, he resembled Daniel who walked
into a den of lions!

This gathering of guests had been premeditated. It was not
a sincere offer of hospitality. The fact that critical lawyers
were present suggests they had already been advised of the
opportunity to question Jesus. The Savior had been addressing an outdoor congregation when the Pharisee invited Him to
dinner, but what apparently was to be a time of fellowship,
eventually became an unpleasant debating session. Jesus, who
had never been a student in any university, was suddenly
confronted by the most astute legal scholars in Palestine. It is
not difficult to visualize the proceedings. The home of the
Pharisee was probably pretentious, with the guests seated either at a table or on cushions on the carpet-covered floor. At
convenient places were large jars filled with water required
for ceremonial cleansing.

"It is not possible to understand the criticism of the Pharisee, nor appreciate the scathing denunciation of Jesus until one has become acquainted with the ridiculous requirements of the man-made laws of the Jews. This was not a casual washing of the hands in normal preparation for a meal. If that had been the point in question, the Lord would not have reprimanded His host in such a way. Many writers have tried to express the details of the ceremonial law but probably Barclay's account is among the most informative. This author in his delightful *Daily Study Bible*, at page 158, says, 'The law laid it down that before a man ate he must wash his hands in a certain way, and that he must also wash them between courses. As usual every littlest detail was worked out. Large stone vessels were specially kept for the purpose because ordinary water might be unclean. The amount of water used must be at least a quarter of a log, that is enough to fill one and a half eggshells. First the water must be poured over the hands, beginning at the tips of the fingers and continuing right up to the wrists. Then the palm of each hand must be cleansed by rubbing the fist of the other into it. Finally, water must again be poured over the hand, this time beginning at the wrist and running right down to the finger tips. To the Pharisee to omit the slightest detail of this was to commit sin.' Thus the beauty of the Mosaic law had been spoiled by man-made additions, and when the Lord failed to comply with the requirements of these ceremonial laws, the watching host began to criticize. It was this unfortunate state of affairs which occasioned the scathing denunciation of Jesus. He reminded His hearers that God is more concerned with the state of a man's heart than with the appearance of his hands. Holiness is a quality within the soul; sin is greater than a speck of dust on the hand. One kind act is of more value in the sight of God than all the ceremonial washing preceding any feast."[1]

Throughout the history of the Hebrew race, the practice of washing before and during meals was mandatory. Every worshiper or guest was expected to comply with the ritual, and to refuse was considered an insult to the entertaining host. When Jesus walked past the water jars without pausing to cleanse His hands, the guests were astonished and whispered their disapproval. "And when the Pharisee saw it, he marveled that he had not first washed before dinner" (Luke 11:38). Jesus understood what the host was thinking and proceeded to utter six "woes" which suggested informative word pictures.

A Startling Contrast . . . *Practical*

And the Lord said unto him, Now do ye Pharisees make clean the outside of the cup and the platter, but your inward part is full of ravening and wickedness (Luke 11:39).

The statement mentioned utensils and dishes which were only partially clean. The outer side had been carefully cleansed, but the inside had been neglected. A servant who was guilty of this would have been severely reprimanded or dismissed from his employment. The Pharisees who had gathered for dinner had meticulously washed their hands but were indifferent regarding the corruption in their souls. This was a terrible indictment against the lawyers who were always seeking faults in other people but remained ignorant of their own depravity. They should have been wiser men, for their Scriptures said: "The LORD seeth not as man seeth; for man looketh on the outward appearance, but the LORD looketh on the heart" (1 Sam. 16:7).

A Special Concern . . . *Predominant*

Woe unto you, Pharisees! for ye love the uppermost seats in the synagogues, and greetings in the markets (Luke 11:43).

The Lord evidently was aware of the conceit of His critics. They were egocentric, desiring the praise of men. When they attended the services in the synagogue, they demanded the most prominent seats so that they could be seen by the entire congregation. Every movement made was meant to attract attention. When beggars at the door asked for alms, the Pharisees looked around to be certain their benevolence was being seen, and the giving of the coin was ostentatiously given. When there were no spectators, the proud man looked away, pretending not to see the beggar. On market days these hypocritical donors wore their most attractive clothing and walked through the crowded streets enjoying the salutations of the crowd, acting as though they were the elite of mankind. They loved to see men bowing as they approached and enjoyed the reactions when grateful beggars loudly thanked their benefactors.

During the time the Savior was in that house His words were as rapier thrusts, cutting through the superficial crust of conceit, hypocrisy, and falsehood. He had been invited to dinner, but possibly the meal was never served. The other guests became so enraged they detested their antagonist. The Lord was concerned, courageous, and challenging. He refused to be intimidated.

A Serious Contamination . . . *Prevailing*

Woe unto you, scribes and Pharisees, hypocrites! for ye are as graves which appear not, and the men that walk over them are not aware of them (Luke 11:44).

Three types of people were invited to the dinner. The Pharisees were there to ask questions, the lawyers to find fault with the Savior, and the scribes to provide written evidence that could be used at future arraignments. They were a nest of vipers! The statement that they were unseen graves was particularly offensive, and the audience had no illusions regarding the insinuation. Defilement was a serious menace which all Hebrews feared. Contact with death prevented entry into important places and deprived people of valued privileges. The law demanded that every grave be clearly marked to warn travelers, and ignoring the regulations was punishable by law. Even the most remote contact with a decaying corpse was considered to be a terrible calamity.

When the Savior accused the guests of being unmarked graves, he made His most serious accusation. They were sources of putrefaction. In spite of their self-esteem they endangered innocent people. The scribes who made notes were writing death warrants for sincere men and women and would be held accountable for their deeds. The lawyers who accused others in a court of law would themselves be judged in God's hall of justice. They professed to be interpreters of the Mosaic law, but did things for which others were condemned. It is not difficult to visualize the Lord pointing an accusing finger in their direction and saying indignantly:

> Woe unto you also, ye lawyers! for he lade men with burdens grievous to be borne, and you yourselves touch not the burdens with one of your fingers. Woe unto you! for ye build the sepulchres of the prophets, and your fathers killed them. Truly ye bear witness that ye allow the deeds of your fathers: for they indeed killed them, and ye build their sepulchres (Luke 11:46–48).

The torrent of words proceeding from the lips of the Lord was devastating, and probably the guests lost their appetites. There were many monuments in Jerusalem which were esteemed by pilgrims. When Jesus said the other guests were hypocrites, He was justified. The religious leaders revered the prophets but, had it been possible, would have repeated the murderous actions of their ancestors.

A Strong Challenge . . . *Presented*

> Woe unto you, lawyers! for ye have taken away the key of knowledge: ye entered not in yourselves, and them that were entering in ye hindered (Luke 11:52).

"The Talmud gives us the clue to the Master's words of bitter reproach here. There were very many in that restless age of inquiry waiting for the consolation of Israel who longed to enter into the real meaning of psalm and prophecy. But the scribe, the lawyer, and the doctor, with their strange and unreal interpretations, their wild and fantastic legends, their own often meaningless additions, effectually hindered all real study of the divine oracles. The Talmud—in the form we now possess it—well represents the teaching of these schools so bitterly censored by the Lord."[2]

The key of knowledge was and still is the inspired Word of

God. The legalists in Israel had replaced the commandments with dictates of their own. Their action had hindered true believers, and it was impossible to differentiate between the true and false. The lawyers resembled unreliable watchmen who failed to warn of impending disaster. When people perished, they would be required to answer for their deplorable conduct.

> And as he said these things unto them, the scribes and the Pharisees began to urge him vehemently, and to provoke him to speak of many things: Laying wait for him, and seeking to catch something out of his mouth, that they might accuse him (Luke 11:53–54).

The guests in the Pharisee's home condemned themselves. The cataracts of unbelief had already closed their eyes to the beauty and grace of the Savior. Deceit and pride had poisoned their souls. Jesus read their thoughts and refused to become a victim of their schemes. When they rejected the Lord, they condemned themselves. All people sooner or later will be confronted and challenged by the claims of Jesus and must either accept or reject His message. Wise people consider this fact.

Luke appeared to be impressed by the occasions when the Lord accepted hospitality. He described at least five times when the Savior dined in various houses (see Luke 4:38; 5:29; 7:36; 14:1; 19:5). It is worthy of note that the writer to the Hebrews said: "Jesus Christ the same yesterday, and to day, and for ever" (Heb. 13:8). The Lord loves to be invited into the homes of His people. If He came in disguise to us, what kind of a welcome would He receive?

---

1. Ivor Powell, *Luke's Thrilling Gospel* (Grand Rapids: Kregel Publications, 1984).

2. *The Pulpit Commentary,* vol. 16 (Peabody, Mass.: Hendrickson Publishers, 1984).

He spake also this parable; A certain man had a fig tree planted in his vineyard; and he came and sought fruit thereon, and found none. Then said he unto the dresser of his vineyard, Behold, these three years I come seeking fruit on this fig tree, and find none; cut it down; why cumbereth it the ground? And he answering said unto him, Lord, let it alone this year also, till I dig about it, and dung it. And if it bear fruit, well; and if not, then after that thou shalt cut it down (Luke 13:6–9).

A house without windows resembles a vault, and a sermon without illustrations seldom commands attention. Even the most boring oration generates interest when the speaker tells a story. Many listeners are too young to understand theology, but none too old to be attracted by an anecdote. A raconteur can enthrall multitudes of listeners. Jesus of Nazareth was the greatest storyteller of all ages. Throughout His ministry He used parables to express everlasting truth. His message about a fig tree in a vineyard provided one of His greatest word pictures. Within four verses He encompassed eternity.

The Special Desire . . . *Glorious*

It stuck out like a sore thumb. No man in his senses would expect to see a fig tree among grapes. The people produced fruit of many kinds but one fact was unchangeable—grapes were grapes, and figs were figs, and if a farmer desired to cultivate both, he did so in different areas. It was refreshing to see vineyards reaching to distant horizons and rewarding to taste the grapes, but to plant a fig tree amid such surroundings was an act of irresponsibility. The Lord had probably seen this situation and described it in His preaching.

Evidently this man liked figs, for otherwise he would not have planted the tree among vines. Maybe he considered the fruit essential for the health of his family. Perhaps the matter was discussed at mealtimes, and since the consensus desired to cultivate figs, he did what was requested. Other men who owned adjacent land probably stared and questioned the wisdom of their neighbor. He smiled at their surprise, but he knew what he was doing. His grapes were destined to be sold in the market, but the figs were for private consumption. Jesus said, "A certain man had a fig tree planted in his vineyard." Thus did the Lord capture the attention of His audience. They wondered what He would make of the situation, for throughout their long history the fig tree had been associated with the Hebrew nation. It was first seen in the garden of Eden, where Adam and Eve took its leaves to make the first garments worn by humans. Later this fruit was made into cakes and brought to David (see 1 Chron. 12:40). The Bible describes how Abigail supplied the king with two hundred cakes of figs during his stay in Hebron (see 1 Sam. 25:18). Hezekiah was cured of a life-threatening disease when a lump of figs was placed as a poultice on a boil (see Isa. 38:21).

An important text is found in Joel 1:7 where God identified Himself with the chosen people. Speaking of a heathen invader, the Lord said: "He hath . . . barked *my fig tree*." An ailing fig tree reminded the nation of God's judgments. It suggested the punishment which fell upon people who displeased Jehovah. When Jesus spoke of one special tree in a vineyard, His audience knew He was speaking indirectly about Israel, the fig tree, which had been placed among the other nations in the world. The Hebrews, who were the apple of God's eye, had been favored throughout their long history. W. E. Shewell Cooper says: "In the East, the fig tree produces two special crops every season. The normal winter fruit ripens in May and June, and the summer figs in late August and September. Sometimes one crop overlaps the other . . . It is possible to pick fruit over nine or ten months of the year."[1]

The Serious Disappointment . . . *Grief*

Fig trees produce a full crop of fruit within three years of planting, and this explains why the farmer said: "These three years I come seeking fruit on this fig tree, and find none" (Luke 13:7). His patience had been exhausted; his time was being wasted. Some teachers consider this to be a veiled reference to the fact that Jesus ministered for three years and presented His generation with an opportunity to cooperate with the Almighty. Unfortunately, "He came unto his own, and his own received him not" (John 1:11).

It is difficult to avoid the conclusion that many Christians resemble the children of Israel. They had no special claim upon the Lord, but for some inscrutable reason He loved them, and gave Himself for them. The poet was correct when he wrote:

> Count your blessings,
> Name them one by one,
> And it will surprise you
> What the Lord hath done.

During times of crisis and temptation, many failed to honor their commitments. Vows were forgotten, promises left unfulfilled, and vital tasks neglected. The Savior predicted that in the past days the love of many would wax cold (see Matt. 24:12). He was concerned because the church at Ephesus left their first love (see Rev. 2:4). The farmer—and God—had special desires concerning their fig trees and planned to enjoy the fruit. It must be a cause for sadness when God is grieved with His people. There is a vast difference between the Jewish nation and the Christian church, but some things are changeless. The Lord cannot be thrilled with anybody who remains a disappointment. It would be to the everlasting credit of every Christian if he considered whether or not he is an unfruitful tree.

The Sad Decision . . . *Gloom*

Cut it down; why cumbereth it the ground? (Luke 13:7).

The owner of the vineyard could not have been criticized for his decision; he had done everything possible to promote growth. All fig trees were able to produce crops within three years of planting. The man said, "These three years I come seeking fruit on this fig tree, and find none." His patience had been admirable; he waited until the tree had sufficient time to be productive. An impatient person might have destroyed the tree earlier. The time of reckoning had now arrived; action could no longer be delayed.

This parable was an indictment against Israel, upon whom God had lavished infinite care. They had failed to respond, and the Lord was running out of patience. It is always a sad moment when the Almighty abandons any person or project. The Jewish nation should have known this fact, for they had suffered both in Egypt and Babylon. David wrote: "Like as a father pitieth his children, so the LORD pitieth them that fear him" (Ps. 103:13). Unfortunately, sometimes even children must be chastised. Solomon said: "He that spareth his rod hateth his son: but he that loveth him chasteneth him betimes" (Prov. 13:24). God's children had become rebellious and defiant. If Hc had remained indifferent, He would have violated His own law. The Savior was justified when He expelled the money changers from the temple and removed the things that had turned the sanctuary into a market. The owner of the vineyard never contemplated judgment until he had given the tree every opportunity to be productive. The Lord also continues to plead with unresponsive people. Jeremiah said: "It is of the Lord's mercies that we are not consumed, because his compassions fail not. They are new every morning: great is thy faithfulness" (Lam. 3:22–23).

The Splendid Determination . . . *Grace*

The dresser of the vineyard represents the Savior to whom God entrusted the care of His property. His request expressed reluctance to destroy the useless tree. A great amount of energy had already been used in its cultivation, and to cease now would be a tragedy. Judgment should be temporarily postponed while the skill of the cultivator be used again. This is one of the greatest pictures of God's grace. It indicates that when Christ abandons a soul, salvation becomes impossible. God said, "My spirit shall not always strive with man," but it is also correct to claim the Holy Spirit never ceases His work if there is any chance of success.

When Simon Peter was about to make his greatest mistake, the Savior said, "Simon, Simon, behold, Satan hath desired to have you, that he may sift you as wheat: But I have prayed for thee, that thy faith fail not; and when thou art converted [*turned back again*], strengthen thy brethren" (Luke 22:31–32). What would have happened to Peter had the Lord not prayed for him? Would he have suffered the fate of the fig tree? Would he have been removed from a place of usefulness? The compelling truth of this parable is the reluctance of the supervisor to permit the destruction of the tree. There is nothing attractive about a dead or dying tree. It is only useful as firewood. Could this be claimed for people upon whom God has lavished His care? It is hard to appreciate the feelings of the husbandman who waited for years in the hope of obtaining fruit. Perhaps it is impossible to know how much the Lord is grieved when He looks at us.

The Sudden Doom . . . *Guilt*

> And if it bear fruit, well: and if not, then after that thou shalt cut it down (Luke 13:9).

There comes a last chance for every person with whom God has dealings, but it should be remembered that final opportunity comes in this world and not in the next. It is significant that Christ issued a threefold warning to His listeners.

> Then said Jesus again unto them, I go my way, and ye shall seek me, and shall die in your sins: whither I go ye cannot come . . . I said therefore unto you, that ye shall die in your sins: for if ye believe not that I am he, ye shall die in your sins (John 8:21–24).

The Lord united two important facts: (1) The possibility of dying unforgiven and (2) the impossibility for such people to reach heaven. It must therefore be understood that since Jesus was returning to His Father in heaven, there had to be another destination for unrepentant souls. It is an undeniable fact that the Scriptures speak of heaven and hell. All preachers speak about the former, but unfortunately we are living in an age when the second is seldom mentioned. The Savior said:

Enter ye in at the strait gate: for wide is the gate, and broad is the way, that leadeth to destruction, and many there be which go in thereat: Because strait is the gate, and narrow is the way, which leadeth unto life, and few there be that find it (Matt. 7:13–14).

It must never be forgotten that the Lord came to earth to save sinners; therefore, *men needed to be saved.* If all are destined to reach heaven safely, Christ only needed to exercise patience, and ultimately He would be able to welcome everybody to a place of eternal bliss. He was very emphatic when He said: "I tell you, Nay; but, except ye repent, ye shall all likewise perish" (Luke 13:3). People who believe the teachings of Scripture know God's books will be opened, and sinners condemned (see Rev. 20:11–15).

The Savior described a man's removal from a royal banquet because he was not wearing a wedding garment. The fellow only had himself to blame, for the king had provided garments for every guest. The foolish man who refused the royal gift must have been splendidly attired and believed he did not need charity. The Lord said:

And when the king came in to see the guests, he saw there a man which had not on a wedding garment. And he said unto him, Friend, How camest thou in hither not having a wedding garment? And he was speechless. Then said the king unto his servants, Bind him hand and foot, and take him away, and cast him into outer darkness (Matt. 22:11–13).

Jesus was not only a raconteur. He was God's spokesman upon earth and meant exactly what He said. When fig trees and people reject God's entreaties, their future can only be in jeopardy. "*Now* is the accepted time; behold, *now* is the day of salvation" (2 Cor. 6:2).

---

1. *The Zondervan Encyclopedia of the Bible,* vol. 2 (Grand Rapids: Zondervan Publishing House, 1976).

SO—THE SHORTEST BIG WORD IN SCRIPTURE

For God so loved the world, that he gave his only begotten
Son, that whosoever believeth in him should not perish,
but have everlasting life (John 3:16).

There were occasions when the men who wrote the Bible could not find words capable of expressing the wonder which filled their souls. For example, when Paul wrote to the Philippians, he said, "the peace of God, which passeth all understanding" (Phil. 4:7). The apostle could speak and write about it, but he only touched the fringe of his topic. He was as a child placing toes into the ocean without understanding the size of the sea. Even the officers sent to apprehend Jesus returned to the authorities with a sense of awe, exclaiming, "Never man spake like this man" (John 7:46).

Since the beginning of time men have tried to explain the magnitude of the love of God, but all remained dissatisfied with their efforts. They were trying to express the inexpressible. Paul, who was one of the greatest exponents of the Christian faith, wrote:

For I am persuaded, that neither death, nor life, nor angels, nor principalities, nor powers, nor things present, nor things to come, Nor height, nor depth, nor any other creature, shall be able to separate us from the love of God, which is in Christ Jesus our Lord (Rom. 8:38–39).

David was apparently overwhelmed with the universality of that love when he wrote:

If I ascend up into heaven, thou art there: If I make my bed in hell, behold, thou art there. If I take the wings of the morning, and dwell in the uttermost parts of the sea; Even there shall thy hand lead me, and thy right hand shall hold me (Ps. 139:8–9).

The writers of the New Testament who were overwhelmed by the same thought eventually discovered the simplicity of the small word "so." It seemed to convey more in a moment than could be expressed in lengthy orations. *Webster's Dictionary* has twenty-four small paragraphs which explain the meaning of this diminutive expression. I remember asking a small child how much she loved her father, and, stretching her arms wide, she replied, "Soooooooo much." That child would have pleased the early Christians.

The Immeasurable Love . . . *"For God* so *loved the world"* (John 3:16)

John was a man of vision, a dreamer, and unlike his colleagues who concentrated on the ministry of their Master, he explored eternity. He supplied no details concerning the birth of Jesus and was content to say Christ came from where He had been. "The Word was made flesh and dwelt among us" (John 1:14). John saw the Lord bringing planets into existence and creating order out of chaos. He said Jesus was the WORD—the eternal expression of the Almighty. Sir James Jeans, the famous astronomer, said, "There are more worlds in space than there are grains of sand on all the beaches of earth." The world possesses great lengths of sandy shores, but it would be difficult to count the grains in a single handful.

It is hard to understand how the Lord created billions of planets by issuing a command and incomprehensible that He should be concerned about insignificant people. He bridged a gap between infinity and time. John was amazed that God could love sinners enough to allow His Son to die on their behalf. How could such affection be described? Should it be called *great love* or the *greatest love?* Should he say it was broader than oceans, higher than the sky, and longer than time? John solved his problem by using the word "SO." When he indicated that God's compassion was greater than every demand made upon it, he wrote: "For God *SO* loved the world." The Lord was capable of loving the unlovely. If it were possible for the world's greatest orator to speak for all eternity about the love of God, so much would still be left unsaid that he would have to begin again with identical results.

One of the greatest attempts to express the love of God was

made by Frederick Lehman who lived from 1868 until 1953. He wrote:

> Could we with ink the ocean fill,
> And were the skies of parchment made;
> Were every stalk on earth a quill,
> And every man a scribe by trade.
> To write the love of God above
> Would drain the ocean dry;
> Nor could the scroll contain the whole,
> Though stretched from sky to sky.
>
> O Love of God, how rich and pure;
> How measureless and strong.
> It shall for evermore endure,
> The saints' and angels' song.

The Impressed Listeners . . . *"And* so *spake"* (Acts 14:1)

And it came to pass in Iconium, that they went both together into the synagogue of the Jews, and so spake, that a great multitude both of the Jews and also of the Greeks believed (Acts 14:1).

Iconium was the capital city of its province. It was situated in the midst of very fertile plains which were irrigated by streams from mountains on three sides of the city. It was a cultural and educational center where Romans, Greeks, and Jews lived in harmony. Caesar had established a garrison of troops there, the Jews built a synagogue, and the educated Greeks played an important part in the management of the community. Religion was varied; the Romans had many gods, the Greeks worshiped Jupiter, and the Hebrews believed in Jehovah. A temple to Jupiter had been erected in the area, and its devotees supported their own priest. During one of their missionary journeys, Paul and Barnabas arrived in the city and attended the Sabbath service. It was customary for the rabbi to encourage strangers to address the congregation, and the missionaries accepted his invitation.

John Kitto says:

"From Antioch in Pisidia, the apostolic travelers turned their steps eastward in the direction of Lycaonia, and traversing the barren uplands, after a journey of ninety-three miles, descended to the plain in which Iconium, the capital of the province stood. Here, mountains whose summits lie in the region of perpetual snow, arise on every side except toward the east, where a plain as flat as the desert of Arabia extends far beyond the reach of the eye. The town was pleasantly situated, and in the midst of luxurious gardens and fertile fields. Imagine Paul entering such a place; clothed in eastern dress; diminutive in stature—slightly lame; with a long thin beard, a bald head, a transparent complexion, bright grey eyes, overhanging eyebrows, a cheerful expression of countenance. His whole appearance was indicative of failing health. Such is the description of him which we find in early literature, which, though not in this respect to be implicitly trusted, yet perhaps conveys to us a good deal which is substantially true. He and his friend Barnabas sat down. After the reading of the lessons from the law and the prophets, the rulers of the synagogue, seeing that these strangers were respectable, thoughtful, devout-looking men, sent to them to enquire if they have any word of exhortation to address to the people. It is still the custom for persons who are not ministers to take part in synagogue service; and we remember hearing an Italian merchant deliver a discourse in a synagogue at Leghorn."[1]

When enemies aroused the anger of the citizens, Paul and Barnabas were compelled to flee to adjacent cities, but many years later the memory of persecution endured in Iconium remained. Writing to Timothy, Paul said, "Persecutions, afflictions, which came unto me at Antioch, *at Iconium*, at Lystra; what persecutions I endured; but out of them all the Lord delivered me" (2 Tim. 3:11). Luke never mentioned anything about Paul's sermon; he was only concerned with the apostle's effectiveness. "They *SO* spake . . . " The preachers were so convincing, that "multitudes both of the Jews and also of the Gentiles believed" (see Acts 14:1).

It is disappointing when preachers speak about the matchless love of God and never exhibit any emotion. Dr. Jowett, the famous English minister, said: "Unless the preacher is stirred by his sermon, it will never inspire a congregation." Many Christians shout at sporting events and almost fight at elections, but they are seldom enthusiastic about the death of the Son of God. These people are enigmas. After one of my evangelistic services in the City Hall, Perth, Australia, an usher overheard two business men discussing the preacher. One said: "What did you think of that? Did you believe what he said?" His colleague replied, "No, but he does!" All pastors should *so* preach, that listeners will become receptive. If street corner salesmen can effectively sell rubbish, ministers should be equally successful as they recommend the greatest message given to men.

The Important Loss . . . *"so great salvation"* (Heb. 2:3)

It may be difficult for Christians to understand the hardships endured by early Jewish believers who lived in an alien world where ruthless enemies were a constant menace. Many who had been attracted to the church watched as neighbors were imprisoned and friends fed to ravenous beasts. It was one thing to hear about the love of a Heavenly Father, but another to explain why he did not intervene to help His devoted children. Why was the Lord slow in aiding His people?

The Jews who had worshiped in the temple were unable to continue, for their sanctuary had been destroyed. Sacrifices were no longer offered, and apparently their entire religious world had collapsed. God did nothing to prevent the catastrophe. The writer to the Hebrews was concerned that people who had been so close to the kingdom of God were in danger of losing their souls. This letter was not only a brilliant exposition of Jewish doctrines; it was also a desperate appeal urging people to be aware of great danger. The readers were reminded how the King of angels had been crucified to put away sin. This was a very great salvation which only heaven could supply.

When Simon Peter preached on the Day of Pentecost he announced to his audience, "Neither is there salvation in any other: for there is none other name under heaven given among men, whereby we must be saved" (Acts 4:12). God's servants emphasized an important fact—"MEN MUST BE SAVED." It was necessary for the Son of God to come to earth, for no other Savior could do what needed to be done. The Hebrews were asked a very important question: "How shall we escape if we neglect *so great salvation?*" It was impossible to answer that question, for there was no way of escape. The Lord said, "If ye die in your sins, where I go ye cannot come." Unless He meant what He said, Jesus was a deceiver. The Savior, in preaching to the people of His generation, said, "Except ye repent, ye shall all likewise perish" (Luke 13:3). Unfortunately, modern congregations dislike that kind of preaching, but nothing can change the fact that these words were spoken by the Lord. People need to be warned of the possible consequences of rejection by God. The Almighty provided this "SO GREAT SALVATION" but it must be accepted by those who need it. To lose such a treasure leads to eternal bankruptcy.

---

1. *Kitto's Daily Bible Illustrations* (Grand Rapids: Kregel Publications, 1984).

Then Jesus said unto them, Verily, verily, I say unto you, Moses gave you not that bread from heaven; but my Father giveth you the true bread from heaven. *For the bread of God is he which cometh down from heaven, and giveth life unto the world. Then said they unto him, Lord, evermore give us this bread. And Jesus said unto them, I am the bread of life: he that cometh to me shall never hunger; and he that believeth on me shall never thirst (John 6:32–35).*

"Within the scope of John's gospel may be discovered Christ's claim to be equal with God. The *ego eimi*, the I AM, the name of God continually makes an appearance, but it is worthy of note that on seven different occasions, the Lord expanded the challenging title. If the Christian life be a pilgrimage through time toward eternity, these verses reveal the requirements for the journey.

(1) '*I am the bread*' (John 6:41). This supplies the strength which every Christian requires as he journeys toward the celestial city.

(2) '*I am the light of the world*' (John 8:12). There is no guarantee that the Christian will always live in sunlight. 'Days of darkness still come o'er me, Sorrow's paths I often tread.' Light from the Lord will shine on the path, for He walks at our side.

(3) '*I am the door*' (John 10:9). This is the access or means of entrance to the royal highway. It is not possible to begin unless one enters at the appointed place.

(4) '*I am the good shepherd*' (John 10:11). Sometimes the journey leads through enemy territory. It will be necessary to wrestle against principalities and powers. Occasionally the dangers may be great but the staff and rod of the Shepherd guarantee safety.

(5) *'I am the resurrection, and the life'* (John 11:25). This supplies the needed power for the journey. Sometimes men grow weary, but 'they that wait upon the Lord shall renew their strength.' Resurrection life may be known throughout the entire pilgrimage.

(6) *'I am the way, the truth, and the life'* (John 14:6). We shall never get lost if we stay close to Him for He is the way. We shall never be confused if we listen to His advice, for He is the guide.

(7) *'I am the true vine'* (John 15:1). We shall neither starve nor waste time on the journey. The Bread will feed us. The Vine will fill us with divine life. Constantly pilgrims will bear fruit to His glory. The walk to the Celestial City will not be burdensome, but a joyous experience of union with Christ."[1]

It would be difficult to decide which of the preceding claims is the most important. They are all simple to understand, concise in meaning, and invaluable to faith. Nevertheless, "I am the bread of life" has made an irresistible appeal to the universal church. It expresses the heart of the Gospel.

Proposition One:
Bread has to be prepared ... *it does not grow on trees*

The Lord said: "I am the bread of life which came down from heaven." His listeners were astonished and replied, "Our fathers did eat manna in the desert; as it is written, He gave them bread from heaven to eat" (John 6:31). When Jesus compared Himself with the manna which fell in the wilderness, His adversaries became angry. The food eaten by the children of Israel did not provide immortality. The people who forfeited their opportunity to enter the Promised Land died in the wilderness. The Hebrews were advised to gather what was needed daily, and although it satisfied their hunger, it did not supply everlasting life.

The Savior claimed to be *the true bread*, and said, "He that cometh to me shall never hunger; and he that believeth on me shall never thirst." The Jews could neither appreciate nor understand such teaching, for Jesus was declaring His preexistence. He was in heaven before coming into the world. Unlike the manna which was available to the twelve tribes, the true bread from heaven enabled people to live eternally. Unfortunately, the people rejected the claim of the Savior and lost the greatest opportunity God could offer.

Bread had to be prepared, for it did not grow on trees, vines, nor any other plant. It came into being when wheat or corn was transformed into flour. Someone saw the need of sustaining life and began baking. Customers who now purchase supplies pay little attention to the work necessary to produce bread. They are content to see, purchase, and eat it. If bakers went on strike, a national emergency would be forthcoming, for bread is necessary for every person in the world. Without it, people die.

The coming of Christ to earth was not an accident. He was the center of a plan conceived in the mind of God before time began. The Almighty knew that a special corn of wheat would fall into the ground and die and make possible the food which guaranteed immortality (see John 12:24). It took all the resources of heaven to provide the Bread of Life. It was planned in the eternal ages when the Word was with God (see John 1:1–2). It seems miraculous that what took so long to produce may be received in a moment. People who partake of it never die.

Proposition Two:
Bread can only be offered for a limited time

The children of Israel were warned that the manna collected each morning would last for one day. That which was gathered on the eve of the Sabbath would last two days. The fact that it was perishable prevented needless greed (see Exod. 16:20). It was remarkable that in spite of the instructions given by Moses, the people were disobedient and, as a result, suffered. God was trying to teach opportunities do not last forever. He provided manna, but they were expected to gather it. There are some things that the Lord will not do for His people.

God was expressing truth relative to the *true bread* who later came from heaven. It was never His intention to compel allegiance. He desires it and will go to great lengths to obtain it, but the Lord never interferes with men's ability to choose. They may accept God's provided salvation or reject it, but remain responsible for their actions. People who postpone acceptance of Christ may one day discover they waited too long! When God said, "Now is the day of salvation," He did not mean *tomorrow*. When an opportunity is presented, people should take it and be grateful. A South African farmer complained about the poor quality of his soil and sold his farm for $25,000. The new owner found and operated a gold mine and became a millionaire. God placed the gold beneath the rocky ridge, but man had to extract it. Opportunity often comes once, but seldom twice.

Proposition Three:
Bread is universally acclaimed ... *it satisfies the hunger of all nations*

It would be difficult to find a country where bread is not needed. Black bread may be obtained in Germany, white in America; brown throughout Europe, and gray in other countries of the world. It is called by different names, has varying shapes and sizes, but whatever the differences may be—it is still *bread*. People of all races need it, for in every country they become hungry, and without it die. A beggar may only possess a crust. A millionaire may own bakeries, but the fact that this commodity is essential is irrefutable. Bread is needed everywhere.

The Savior knew this when He instructed the disciples to go into all the world to preach the Gospel to every creature. He said, "He that believeth and is baptized shall be saved, but he that believeth not, shall be damned." Baptism was the appointed method by which Christians testified they had received the Bread of Life. The New Testament churches knew nothing of unbaptized believers. When a man received Christ as his Savior, immersion always followed (see Acts 8:35–38). It is significant that when Mark wrote of salvation he mentioned faith and baptism, but when he spoke of a person being lost, he only mentioned *faith*. "He that believeth not shall be damned." Baptism was only an ordinance, evidence of obedience to the command of Christ. Unfortunately, certain sections of the modern church have rejected that teaching. Some even teach that without baptism, faith is useless. It cannot be overemphasized that water, whether it be applied by pouring, sprinkling, or immersion, cannot wash away sin. Only the precious blood of Christ can perform that miracle. It is wise to remember that bread cannot save nor sustain life unless it be received and eaten. Christ cannot help anyone unless He is received by faith into the human soul.

The Lord commissioned His disciples to go into all the world to preach the Gospel, for without the Bread of Life unevangelized people would suffer irreparable loss. A church that has no missionary program is not pleasing to the Lord. Closed hands are indicative of hearts not open to the leading of God's Spirit. The Bible says, "Give and it shall be given unto you." People who refrain from helping others invariably die poor!

Proposition Four:
Bread sustains health and promotes growth

This was the most astounding sermon ever preached in the synagogue at Capernaum. It surprised many of Christ's followers and annoyed the regular worshipers who became angry when the Lord said:

> I am the living bread which came down from heaven: if any man eat of this bread, he shall live for ever: and the bread that I will give is my flesh, which I will give for the life of the world (John 6:51).

The Savior explained the bread from heaven was His body which would be sacrificed for all nations. While He ministered in Palestine, the Lord, for the most part, only reached a limited number of people. After His resurrection, the Gospel was preached in every part of the world.

It was difficult for the inhabitants of Nazareth to accept the Lord's claim that He had been in heaven before residing in Nazareth and had lived before Adam. The congregation must have thought he had taken leave of His senses. The Savior also indicated that the people who came to Him would return for additional supplies. The living bread would be so delightful that those who ate it would be unable to live without Him. When Jesus broke and blessed the small loaves supplied by a lad, there was enough for everybody.

I remember standing before a Christian leper in Central Africa. His testimony had helped to transform many tribesmen. I asked what was his favorite Bible story, and after a short pause he replied, "I like the story of the feeding of the five thousand. When Jesus broke the bread, there was enough for everybody—if they would take it."

1. Ivor Powell, *John's Wonderful Gospel* (Grand Rapids: Kregel Publications, 1983).

THE SAVIOR—WHO OFTEN
SPOKE ABOUT HIMSELF

What sayest thou? (John 8:5).

When I was sixteen years of age, I was asked to preach in my home church. It was an honor for which I was unprepared. At the end of the service an elder said, "Son, avoid the letter 'I'; don't speak so much about yourself!" Unfortunately, at that time, I had very little Bible knowledge and no experience of what was necessary to be an effective preacher. Many years later I became an author, and I remembered the old man's statement. The continual use of the letter "I" might suggest the speaker possesses an inflated ego. Authors of repute prefer to write: "This author thinks," or "This author believes," etc. It is better and wiser to focus attention on a theme or the characters connected with it. Unless a personal testimony is to be presented, it is wise to avoid expressions which might be detrimental to the message. It is worthy of attention that Jesus of Nazareth was an exception to this rule. Apparently John was the only disciple aware that Jesus consistently spoke about Himself.

The fourth Gospel reveals how Jesus said:

I am the Messiah (John 4:25–26).
I am that bread of life (John 6:48).
I am the light of the world (John 8:12).
I am the door (John 10:7).
I am the good shepherd (John 10:14).
I am the way (John 14:6).
I am the truth (John 14:6).
I am the life (John 14:6).
I am the vine (John 15:5).
I am—GOD! (John 18:5).

There were reasons why the Lord did this. Earlier the prophets predicted His coming to earth, and later the apostles repeated what Christ taught. The Savior claimed He was the only way by which sinners could approach God. There was no other spokesman capable of explaining that fact. If Christ had remained silent, the Gospel of the grace of God would never have been heard. It is important to remember Jesus constantly directed men and women to Himself, saying, "Come unto me, all ye that labour and are heavy laden, and I will give you rest" (Matt. 11:28). Sermons which do not introduce listeners to Christ are uninspired. Miss Fanny Crosby wrote delightful words.

> Tell me the story of Jesus,
> Write on my heart every word;
> Tell me the story most precious,
> Sweetest that ever was heard.
> Tell how the angels, in chorus,
> Sang as they welcomed His birth,
> "Glory to God in the highest!
> Peace and good tidings to earth."

> Tell of the Cross where they nailed Him,
> Writhing in anguish and pain;
> Tell of the grave where they laid Him,
> Tell how He liveth again.
> Love in that story so tender,
> Clearer than ever I see:
> Stay, let me weep while you whisper,
> Love paid the ransom for me.

Every claim made by the Savior was of the utmost importance, but when some of them are considered in sequence, it becomes easy to understand the significance of His remarks.

I Am the Door . . . *How Significant (John 10:9)*

There was only one door in a sheepfold. The walls were sufficiently high to exclude marauding beasts. When the Savior delivered this message, every listener understood the significance of His words. If the sheepfold were the home of the sheep, the kingdom of God was the true sanctuary of God's sheep. Jesus said: "I am the way, the truth, and the life: *No man cometh unto the Father, but by me*" (John 14:6).

Deluded people insist there are many ways by which to enter God's kingdom. It is said that Muslims, Buddhists, and other people can reach heaven by observing their own religious rites. It cannot be overemphasized that these doctrines are false. Jesus taught He was the only door of the sheepfold. The apostle Peter emphasized also that fact when he said: "Neither is there salvation in any other: for *there is none other name* under heaven given among men, whereby we must be saved" (Acts 4:12).

I Am the Good Shepherd . . . *How Supportive (John 10:11)*

Within a land where shepherds and their flocks could be seen every day, it was to be expected that Jesus would refer to them. His example was followed by the disciples, who throughout their ministry, referred to Christ as the Shepherd of God's sheep. Jesus called Himself *the good shepherd.* The writer to the Hebrews said He was *the great shepherd* (Heb. 13:20). The apostle Peter stated Christ was *the chief shepherd (1 Peter 5:4).* There appears to be an interesting development in the three expressions. A good shepherd might be any man intensely devoted to his flock. A great shepherd seems to imply distinction of service, skill in finding excellent pasture, and bravery in defending the flock. When the Lord was named *the chief shepherd*, the apostle ascribed to Him an honor not shared with another. As Paul wrote: "He was far above all" (see Eph. 4:10).

The Savior spoke of thieves and robbers who could not be trusted. They brought death, whereas He came to give life, and life more abundant (see John 10:10). The sheep not only recognized the voice of their shepherd, they were content to follow Him. The Lord also mentioned hirelings who accepted responsibility for services never rendered. They quit their post whenever more lucrative employment became available. Jesus said, "They cared not for the sheep." It is difficult to avoid the conclusion that their kind are still living! Jesus was never a shepherd; He worked in a carpenter's shop, but nevertheless,

159

His early years were spent in a locality where sheep were a vital part of daily life. When in spare moments He walked in the fields, His eyes became misty, for He was destined to become the Shepherd who would lay down His life for the sheep. He said: "And other sheep I have, which are not of this fold: them also I must bring, and they shall hear my voice; and there shall be one fold, and *one shepherd*" (John 10:16). Christ anticipated the time when He would be the Leader of God's international flocks, and the song of all believers would be

Where He leads me, I will follow.

I Am the Light of the World . . . *How Sufficient (John 8:12)*

This statement was a bright star shining in a very dark sky. A desperate woman had been accused of committing adultery, and her captors were desirous of an immediate execution. Jesus had thwarted their plan, and completely amazed, she stared into the face of her Benefactor. It was difficult to believe that the arrogant Jews had gone away. Then the Lord said, "Woman, where are those thine accusers? hath no man condemned thee? She said, No man, Lord. And Jesus said unto her, Neither do I condemn thee: go, and sin no more" (John 8:10–11). Afterward the Savior said, "I am the light of the world: he that followeth me shall not walk in darkness, but shall have the light of life" (John 8:12).

Had any other man uttered those words, he would have become an object of scorn. Throughout history several misguided leaders desired to rule the world, but everybody knows what happened to them. Yet Jesus, who had no armies to support His cause, no bank balance from which to pay expenses, and no organization to advertise His virtue ultimately proved what He claimed to be. The story of His birth, life, death, and resurrection has thrilled all nations. Cannibals have been transformed, criminals changed by the power of divine love, and outcasts so influenced, they devoted their lives to His cause. The light of the Gospel shines throughout the world, and someday all nations will worship at His feet. It can be truthfully said:

The people that walked in darkness have seen a great light: they that dwell in the land of the shadow of death, upon them hath the light shined (Isa. 9:2).

During my stay in Africa, I spoke with a Zulu one day and asked how many cows he would have to pay for the daughter of a chief. Rolling his eyes and lifting his arms, he replied, "Oooo, anyt'ing up to fifty." I looked with a smile at that fellow, Samuel, and told him that perhaps, after all, his people were better off than the Europeans. He was so puzzled I had to explain what I meant.

"Samuel, you pay to get a wife. The white man pays because he's 'got' one." He thought for a moment, then his radiance shone forth, and he said, "Tha's so, Master, tha's so."

"Samuel," I said, "I know of Another who had to buy his wife. Once there was a great Man who so loved poor sinners that He wanted to 'marry' them. He wanted them to be near Him for ever. His name was Jesus, and He wanted a church as His Bride—but He had to buy her. Yes, He was very wealthy, for the Bible—the white man's book—says that every beast of the forest is His, and the cattle upon a thousand hills. Yet all His cattle were not enough to pay for His bride. He had to pay a greater price. Samuel, do you know what He had to do?"

"Yes, Master, He had to give Himself—He died for us." I marveled as I listened, for at that moment, into the boy's eyes came an exquisite tenderness. I wondered what David Livingstone would have said had he been present.

I Am . . . the Truth . . . *How Substantiated (John 14:6)*

Within a world of conflicting ideas it is sometimes difficult to recognize truth. Teams of eloquent lawyers argue against each other, and enormous sums of money are spent trying to ascertain what is true and what is false. This is very evident among religious people. Since the beginning of the Christian era, men disputed the claims of Christ, and successive editions of the Scriptures claimed to be superior to predecessors.

161

When conflicting opinions are expressed, people generally say, "It is a matter of interpretation." It is sometimes difficult to decide which of the ideas is correct. When Jesus stood before Pilate, He was asked, "What is truth?" When Pharisees and Sadducees argued, ordinary citizens hardly knew what to believe. Jesus said, "I am the truth," and stated a fact which has endured through time. He was the embodiment of truth, the Spokesman for the Almighty. What He taught was meant to be the standard by which all opinions would be accepted or rejected. When His authority is ignored, stability and reason are destroyed. The claim made by the Savior has been substantiated in various ways.

When the Lord was upon the Mount of Transfiguration, "Behold a voice out of the cloud, which said, This is my beloved Son, in whom I am well pleased; *hear ye him*" (Matt. 17:5). God endorsed the teaching of Christ because, as John said, Jesus was *THE WORD* (see John 1:1–2, 14). The only function for a word is the conveyance of thought. Jesus was the means by which God revealed Himself. What was expressed was written, and the Bible became a light shining in the world's darkness. If nations would listen to, and obey, the instructions of the Almighty, earth's problems would disappear.

I Am the True Vine . . . *How Sustaining (John 15:1)*

Palestine was filled with vineyards; people worked in them every day. The prosperity of the nation depended upon the production of grapes. When Jesus stated He was THE TRUE VINE, He suggested many things. As the husbandman devoted his attention to the cultivation of fruit, so God was supportive of everything done by the Savior. The Lord said, "My Father is the husbandman" (John 15:1), and He referred to the words of the psalmist who compared Israel to a vine planted by Jehovah (see Ps. 80:8). The Savior emphasized that He was the *true* vine; all others were insignificant.

Christ was the Vine which drew nourishment from inexhaustible rivers. Jesus taught that every believer was a branch through which His life could flow. The entire plan of salvation was expressed in this parable. God was in charge of the operation. Jesus was the Vine through which the Almighty perfected His plans. The branches were used in the production of fruit which would enrich the nations. Jesus never hesitated to state His claim, for this was a fact that needed to be publicized.

I Am ... God! ... *How Strong (John 18:5–6)*

Jesus therefore, knowing all things that should come upon him, went forth, and said unto them, whom seek ye? They answered him, Jesus of Nazareth. Jesus saith unto them, I AM ... As soon then as he had said unto them I AM, they went backward, and fell to the ground (John 18:4–6).

Throughout His ministry, by word and deed, Jesus indicated He was infinitely more than a mere man; He claimed to be equal with God. The Jewish people denied that fact, but they had no illusions about His message. Their accusation before Pilate was self-explanatory. "He ought to die, because he made himself the Son of God" (John 19:7). There were, and still are, men and movements which deny the deity of Christ, but the people who crucified the Lord clearly understood His words. It is interesting to observe that when they charged Him with blasphemy, *He never denied the accusation*, for it was true. He did make Himself equal with the Almighty. The apostle John wrote:

In the beginning was the Word, and the Word was with God, and the Word *was* God. ... And the Word was made flesh, and dwelt among us, and we beheld his glory, the glory as of the only begotten of the Father, full of grace and truth (John 1:1, 14).

The greatest endorsement of the claims of Christ was provided in the Garden of Gethsemane, when a large crowd was overwhelmed by a manifestation of divine power. When the Lord confronted His enemies, His majesty shone through the barrier of flesh and the glory of the Almighty overwhelmed the forces of evil. Centuries earlier, Moses asked for evidence to prove he had been authorized to deliver Israel, and God said, "Tell them the I AM sent you" (see Exod. 3:13–14). A former President of the United States of America, Ronald Regan, was correct when he said, "If Jesus of Nazareth were not what He claimed to be, He was the greatest charlatan who ever lived." Any diligent student can count the occasions when Jesus used a personal pronoun to enhance His claims. What He said was so vital that had He remained silent, even the stones would have protested! (see Luke 19:40).

SIMON PETER AND HIS GREAT FISHING STORIES

Simon Peter saith unto them, I go a fishing (John 21:3).

The well-known pianist, Arthur Rubinstein, who spoke fluently in eight languages, told how he was afflicted with a severe cold and hoarseness. When none of the usual remedies gave relief, he made an appointment to see a throat specialist. He said, "I searched his face for a clue during the thirty-minute examination, but it was without expression. He told me to come back the next day, so I went home filled with fears and did not sleep that night. The following day there was another prolonged test and once again it was accompanied by an ominous silence. At last I could stand it no longer and said to the doctor: 'Tell me, what is the matter? I can stand the truth; I have lived a full, rich life. What is wrong with me?' The specialist replied, 'You talk too much!'"

One wonders what that doctor might have said to Simon Peter who was a prolific talker! When God controlled the man's speech, blessings followed; when He did not, trouble could be expected. The Big Fisherman, as he has often been called, usually acted in haste and repented at leisure. At the fire on the night of Christ's arrest a maid terrorized him. Yet when he preached on the Day of Pentecost, Simon was God's man for the moment. He was the most interesting of all the disciples, and if it were possible to engage him in conversation, his fishing stories would be enthralling. Christians are attracted to him, for they see what they would like to become and in his mistakes, the reflection of what they are. The Lord was also interested in the exploits of Peter and decreed that some of his remarkable fishing stories should be included in the archives of eternity.

The Fisherman Who Listened . . . *Realizing the Truth*

And when they had this done, they inclosed a great multitude of fishes: and their net brake. And they beckoned unto their partners, which were in the other ship, that they should come and help them. And they came and filled both the ships, so

165

that they began to sink. When Simon Peter saw it, he fell down at Jesus' knees, saying, Depart from me; for I am a sinful man, O Lord (Luke 5:6–8).

Huge rivers begin with small streams, and some of the greatest church leaders came from unpretentious beginnings. The apostle Peter was a native of Bethsaida, a city close to the Sea of Galilee. He and his brother, Andrew, were fishermen. Their partners, James and John, also owned a boat, and the four men were well-known in the area. Simon became a leader of the Christian church and was God's spokesman on the Day of Pentecost. Later in his life he wrote two epistles that were included in the canon of Holy Scripture.

This interesting character first met Jesus of Nazareth when his brother Andrew said, "We have found the Messiah." That startling announcement encouraged Simon to seek the cause of the excitement. Later the Lord attended a service in the synagogue at Capernaum and went into Peter's home to heal his sick mother-in-law. The fisherman was greatly impressed by the Savior's work and was prepared for the morning when he allowed the Lord to borrow his boat. If Simon Peter were on earth today he might say:

"I shall never forget the morning when my brother and I were attending to our nets. We had been fishing all night, had caught nothing, and were damp, frustrated, and tired. We had cast our nets and pulled them in again and again until our arms ached. It seemed as if all the fish were hiding. Neither my brother nor I could understand what had happened. Then we saw a crowd coming along the beach and recognized they were following Jesus. We had not forgotten His visit to our home, and when He asked for the use of the boat, it was a pleasure to grant His request. Hastily, we launched the ship to take it out a short distance and, releasing the anchor, sat back expectantly.

"When Jesus began to speak, I was enthralled. Yet, as He continued, I began to feel uncomfortable. He seemed to be speaking to me. I felt as if I were in a trance, but when I came to my senses, He was smiling. He wanted to go for a ride.

Then He asked me to let down the nets, but that seemed foolish. As I had told Him, we had been fishing all night and had caught nothing. I thought the suggestion to be ridiculous, but if it would provide pleasure, He could see how we operated.

"He watched as we threw out a net. I had the shock of my life, for when we commenced to trawl, fish were jumping everywhere. They were swimming into our net as if they were all committing suicide. The fish were heavy, and our vessel began to sink. I yelled to our partners in the other boat, and they came to help, but it became obvious that unless we got back to shore quickly, the catch and our equipment would be lost.

"It was too much for me; I could only stare at the Savior as shame overwhelmed my soul. I knelt and said, 'Depart from me, for I am a sinful man, O Lord.' I shall never forget the gleam in His eyes when He said, 'Fear not, from henceforth thou shalt catch men!' I was ecstatic. The other men attended to the fish, but I only had one desire—to follow Jesus. My brother, Andrew, was correct when he said, 'We have found the Messiah, the Savior of the world.'"

Perhaps Simon Peter would understand the sentiments expressed by an unknown author.

> My Pastor shapes his sermons
> From A to final Z.
> In clear and forthright language,
> And aims them straight at me.
>
> And when he gets to preaching,
> I look around to see
> If there might be another
> Deserving more than me.
>
> But every soul looks saintly,
> Their hearts to heaven turn,
> While I in my conviction
> Can only turn and squirm.

167

You know, I often wonder
If I should miss a day,
Would he without his target,
Have anything to say?

The Fisherman Who Learned... *Raising the Taxes*

And when they were come to Capernaum, they that received
tribute money came to Peter, and said, Doth not your master
pay tribute? He saith, Yes (Matt. 17:24).

"If I were asked to describe the strangest event in my fishing
career, I would have to tell of the fish who helped pay my tax.
It happened in Capernaum where an official asked if Jesus
ever paid taxes. Maybe he wondered if the Master paid in
Jerusalem or Capernaum; or perhaps he inquired if the Lord
had some special exemption. Without thinking I replied, 'Yes,'
but afterward I wondered if I had been truthful. I had no
recollection of Jesus going to a tax collector, and the thought
worried me. Of course, I could not hide my feelings from the
Lord, and it was difficult to be silent when He asked what
was troubling me. It was strange when He said princes were
not required to pay taxes. He said:

'Notwithstanding, lest we should offend them, go thou to the
sea, and cast an hook, and take up the fish that first cometh
up; and when thou hast opened his mouth, thou shalt find a
piece of money: that take, and give unto them for me and
thee' (Matt. 17:27).

"I went down to the edge of the sea, baited and cast in the
hook, and almost immediately caught a fish. When I opened
its mouth, I saw a Greek coin which was worth a shekel or
two drachmas. It was sufficient to pay the tax for two people.
For a moment I was amazed and could not believe my eyes.
Of course I paid the taxes, but now I wish I had kept that
coin. I should have paid in some other way. I told the Master
what had happened but could not forget His words: 'For me
and thee.' That was my greatest fishing experience."

168

The world now knows it was not unusual to find a coin in such a place. A fish might seize anything bright which is dropped into the sea. Dr. H. D. M. Spence tells of a cod which was caught with a watch in its stomach—*"still going."* The true miracle of this fish was twofold: (1) The Lord knew the coin would be found in the *first* fish to take Peter's hook and (2) He knew the value of the coin; it would be sufficient to pay tax for two people. "For me and thee."

"Yes," said Simon Peter, "That was a strange moment. How could the Master know so much? There were millions of fish in the lake, but He knew a coin had been dropped and recovered by one special fish which He commanded to seize the tempting bait. This was arranged to fit into His timetable. Every time afterward when I caught a fish, instinctively, I looked into its mouth wondering if I would find another coin! I never did and should have known the Lord supplies *our needs*, not *our wants*. I needed to learn that lesson."

The Fisherman Who Loved . . . *Repeating the Testimony*

There were together Simon Peter, and Thomas called Didymus, and Nathanael of Cana in Galilee, and the sons of Zebedee, and two other of his disciples. Simon Peter saith unto them, I go a fishing. They say unto him, We also go with thee. They went forth, and entered into a ship immediately; and that night they caught nothing (John 21:2–3).

Simon Peter paused. A faraway look came into his eyes. It seemed he was reliving the past. After the resurrection of the Lord, he said to his colleagues, "I go a fishing." The other men replied, "We also go with thee." "Well," said Simon, "What else was there to do? Life had ended for us when the Master died and commenced again when He arose. But He was different, and we were fearful of the future. If He went away again, we had to earn a living and support our families. I knew how to fish; in fact that was about all I did know. We would always have cherished memories of the Lord, but we could not sit still hoping for something to happen.

"My brothers agreed with my suggestion. Judas was gone.

169

Some of the others were absent, but the rest of us went down to the shoreline, took two boats, and proceeded to the fishing grounds. It was hard work, but although we pulled our nets in again and again, we caught nothing. It was frustrating. It had happened before, but then Jesus was with us, and He had the ability to turn failure into success. Finally, reason prevailed, and we returned to shore. As we approached the beach we saw a man whom we supposed to be a merchant. He asked about the catch, and we told Him we had nothing to see. He advised us to cast the net on the right side of the ship, and for some inexplicable reason we did as He suggested. Soon, we had one hundred and fifty and three large fish. I know, because I counted them. John was the first to recognize the Master, but when I reached the shore, I saw He had lit a fire and cooked our breakfast. The stillness of the morning was unbroken except for the noise of waves on the beach. Suddenly I heard the Master saying, 'Simon Son of Jonas, lovest thou me more than these?' For a few moments I wondered what He meant. He seemed to be looking at my companions and the fish. I remembered that awful night when I disowned Him and felt too ashamed to reply. But His compelling eyes were focused on me, and I whispered, 'Yes, Lord. I certainly do.'

"It was very embarrassing when He asked the same question three times. Maybe *He likes us to tell Him that we love Him.* Occasionally we get so involved in current events we forget to say what He deserves to hear. When He gave me a new commission, it was difficult to believe. He was willing to trust me again. I never forgot that morning, for it was the last time I went fishing. He asked me to look after His flock, and that has been a full-time job. Actually, He gave to me two tasks. He made me a fisher of men, but each catch makes my work a little more difficult. My fish become sheep. I sometimes wonder what happened to our boats. Do the new owners ever go fishing in vain? Jesus asked if I loved Him, but ever since I have striven to make the question unnecessary."

I, even I, am the LORD; and beside me there is no savior (Isa. 43:11).

Neither is there salvation in any other: for there is none other name under heaven given among men, whereby we must be saved (Acts 4:12).

The prophet Isaiah ministered during one of the most decadent and dangerous periods in Israel's history. The Jews had abandoned the laws of God and were a nation of idolaters. Prophets had been killed and the warnings of Jehovah, ignored. Believers who desired to be faithful to Jehovah, were persecuted, and lawlessness prevailed throughout the land. Idols were worshiped, and even along the highways were shrines where travelers could pause and pay homage. The Lord did everything possible to bring people to repentance but He failed, and finally the Babylonians were permitted to subjugate the country. Many defenders were either killed in battle or taken as prisoners to an alien land where they learned to detest images. Repeatedly Jehovah spoke saying, "I, even I, am the Lord; and beside me there is no Savior," but the people refused to listen—preferring their silent idols to a God who continually complained about their conduct.

God Is Jealous ... *He can be hurt*

America has often been compared with the ancient world. Although the Word of God has been faithfully proclaimed, multitudes refuse to listen. The One whom our fathers worshiped has been replaced by man-made idols. Within this favored country it is now possible to find every type of religion. Temples which once only existed in India, Burma, China, and Japan now occupy prominent places in the western world. Beneath the banner of free speech anybody can say anything. Nevertheless, the real gods of the western world are not made of wood nor carved from stone. They are deities enthroned within the souls of their devotees. Multitudes worship money, sex, and sport. An athlete who can throw or kick a ball may become an object of veneration and is bigger than politics. He can receive in one week more money than a president can earn in a year!

There are many places where it is unsafe to walk after dark, for men act like animals. Women are attacked, raped, and often murdered. Unfortunately, people have become accustomed to these sordid deeds. They read about them in the newspapers, shrug their shoulders, and forget the anguish suffered by victims. Vice has turned cities into places of terror; drugs and alcohol have ruined society. Preachers denounce such practices, but most people remain indifferent.

When Jesus was upon the earth, He said, "But as the days of Noah were, so shall also the coming of the Son of man be. For as in the days that were before the flood, they were eating and drinking, marrying and giving in marriage, until the day that Noah entered into the ark. And knew not until the flood came, and took them all away; so shall also the coming of the Son of man be" (Matt. 24:37–39). The Savior was correct in His assessment, and if He were here today, He would emphasize the same message. Isaiah repeated that salvation came only from the Almighty. His words need to be heard in every nation. Israel rejected that message and perished. History has an unpleasant way of repeating itself. Sinners who ignore the warnings of God are in danger. When God finally rejects a nation or an individual, there is no court of appeal. Blessed are they who with David can say: "Some trust in chariots, and some in horses: but we will remember the name of the LORD our God" (Ps. 20:7).

God Is Just ... *He must be fair*

Tell ye, and bring them near; yea, let them take counsel together: who hath declared this from ancient time? who hath told it from that time? have not I the LORD? and there is no God else beside me; a just God and a Saviour; there is none beside me. Look unto me, and be ye saved, all the ends of the earth; for I am God, and there is none else (Isa. 45:21–22).

172

God is obligated to His laws. If He violated the commandments, He would become a sinner as did Adam and Eve. The Lord said that if a watchman failed to warn citizens of approaching danger, he would be responsible for the fate of the community (see Ezek. 33:6). The divine guardian of Israel was aware of approaching danger. If human watchmen were responsible for remaining silent, God would have been blamed for not warning sinners of their peril.

Earlier in his ministry Isaiah said: "Come now, and let us reason together, saith the LORD: though your sins be as scarlet, they shall be as white as snow; though they be red like crimson, they shall be as wool" (Isa. 1:18). God's invitation was not accepted, and He was compelled to use other methods. Patience was extremely commendable, but since Jehovah had said, "My spirit shall not always strive with man" (Gen. 6:3), it was incumbent upon the Lord to honor His word. Through Isaiah, He said: "I have sworn by myself, and *the word is gone out of my mouth in righteousness*" (Isa. 45:23). God's predictions will be fulfilled. Souls who cooperate will be forgiven; others will perish.

Mankind had been taught from *ancient times*, therefore Israel had no excuse for ignorance. The people who rejected Noah's message died in the waters of the flood. Sinners who do likewise with the Gospel must suffer the consequences of their deeds. Since the dawn of time, God has insisted that He is the Sovereign of the universe. Other gods, idols, or images would not be tolerated. Unfortunately, the children of Israel ignored that claim, and rejecting the warning, became slaves. These facts are irrefutable, but human folly continues. The Hebrews never valued Jehovah's help until it was denied. They learned more in Babylon than they did in the temple at Jerusalem.

God Is Jesus . . . *He desires to help*

In the beginning was the Word, and the Word was with God, and the Word was God. The same was in the beginning with God (John 1:1–2).

173

> And the Word was made flesh, and dwelt among us, and we beheld his glory, the glory as of the only begotten of the Father, full of grace and truth (John 1:14).

Israel's God decided to put on garments of humanity so that John and others could say: "That which was from the beginning, which we have heard, which we have seen with our eyes, which we have looked upon, and our hands have handled, of the Word of life. For the life was manifested, and we have seen it" (1 John 1:1–2). The beloved disciple included other disciples in his claim. He spoke of *us* and said, "*We* have seen it." Peter repeated the same truth on the Day of Pentecost. He knew what was taught in the synagogues and was aware of what the prophets had said. They repeated that God was their only Savior. The apostle also said, "Neither is there salvation in any other: for there is none other name under heaven given among men, whereby we must be saved" (Acts 4:12).

The entire world needs to examine the words of Jesus, for unless He were what He claimed to be, He was a liar misleading listeners.

It was significant that throughout His ministry Jesus was unequaled in His announcements and achievements; no other person could be compared with Him. An official who was sent to arrest Him said, "Never man spake like this man" (John 7:46). The Savior's ability to impart truth superseded that of any prophet. The others repeated what they were told; Jesus spoke for Himself. They needed inspiration; the Lord did not. He was always responsible for His own statements. Even children understood His message, and yet His words were so profound, even Israel's learned critics were silenced.

No other could be compared with the Prince of glory. That assertion could also be made concerning His achievements. Blind eyes were opened, lepers cleansed, the dead were raised. This fact brought the eminent Nicodemus to interview the Lord. The greatest teacher in Israel knew the time for the Messiah's appearance had passed. If the prophet had spoken accurately, the Anointed One would already have grown to manhood. Nicodemus was asking a question—"If Jesus were not the Messiah, who was?" There was no other person who possessed the necessary qualifications.

The apostle Peter was aware of all these details, and when he addressed the crowd in Jerusalem he emphasized the fact that *"there was none other name . . .* whereby men must be saved." It was evident to everybody that if Jesus were removed, a substitute could not be found. God had clothed Himself with humanity, had walked among men, and was "in Christ, reconciling the world unto himself" (see 2 Cor. 5:19).

It is to be regretted that liberal theologians have denied this important truth. They suggest that as there are twelve entrances to the New Jerusalem, so there are many ways by which people can approach God. All non-Christians believe they will be accepted by the Almighty, but that refutes the teaching of Jesus. If all nations will safely reach God's country, why should the Lord instruct His disciples to evangelize the world? If heathens were already safe, it was unnecessary to dispatch missionaries and spend vast sums of money to finance something which was needless.

The Lord said: "I am the way, the truth, and the life: *no man cometh unto the Father, but by me"* (John 14:6). Buddha, Mohammed, and the leaders of other religions cannot save, but JESUS THE SON OF GOD CAN. He is the Jehovah of the Old Testament, the Redeemer of the New Testament. He is from everlasting to everlasting, the unchanging Savior of the world.

> But this man, because he continueth ever, hath an unchangeable priesthood. Wherefore he is able also to save them to the uttermost that come unto God by him, seeing he ever liveth to make intercession for them (Heb. 7:24–25).

When this letter was sent to the Jews of his generation, the writer hoped to dispel fears of the future. The destruction of the temple had left people bewildered and apprehensive. If Christianity failed they had nothing left upon which to reply. Priests no longer ministered, and sacrifices had been discontinued. The people could be left sinking in quicksands of uncertainty. Many theologians believe this writer was Paul, that his letter represented the type of sermon preached in the synagogues. This identification, though interesting, is not of importance. Evangelical Christians believe the author was only a human pen in the hand of God.

The Aaronic priests could not complete what they commenced, but Christ continues indefinitely. He was already enthroned at the right hand of God. He who had commenced the work of redemption would conclude it triumphantly. The statement made in Hebrews 7:28 was an appeal to despondent believers to place their trust in the one and only Savior, the Lord Jesus Christ, the Son of the Living God!

> Yes, all the griefs He felt were ours,
> Ours were the woes He bore;
> Pangs not His own, His spotless soul,
> With bitter anguish tore.
>
> He died to bear the guilt of men,
> That sin might be forgiven.
> He lives to bless them, and defend,
> And plead their cause in heaven.

PAUL—WHO MAY HAVE HAD
A WONDERFUL SISTER

Salute Andronicus and Junia, my kinsmen, and my fellow prisoners, who are of note among the apostles, who also were in Christ before me (Rom. 16:7).

The epistle to the Romans is widely recognized as one of the most important letters written by Paul. It is constructive, corrective, and at its conclusion, intensely appreciative. If the eleventh chapter of Hebrews can be called "God's Art Gallery of Faith," the sixteenth chapter of Romans may be named "Paul's Album of Special Friends." The apostle specially mentioned twenty-nine people. Probably many of these met Paul during his missionary journeys and who for reasons unknown, were then residing in Rome. The apostle, who planned to visit the imperial city, did not wish to leave anyone out of his letter and sent greetings to his special friends.

His reference to Andronicus and Junia has caused endless discussion among the churches. He also said Herodion was a kinsman (see Rom. 16:11). Some commentators have expressed the opinion these people were Jews, but that is difficult to accept since the others cited were also Hebrews. It would be strange if they were all merely Jews when Paul only named three as members of his family. The apostle had a sister and nephew who were either residents of Jerusalem or visiting the city when his life was being threatened (see Acts 23:16).

Whether Junia was a sister, cousin, or a distant relative does not alter the fact this person was related to the apostle. The fact that Paul had a sister in Jerusalem supports the idea that he stayed in her home during the time when he was one of Gamaliel's students.

Dr. Herbert Lockyer believed the lady and her son might have been on vacation in the city when the lad informed the officer of the plot to murder his uncle. Some teachers believe the two people to whom Paul sent greetings were men, cousins of the apostle, but as Matthew Henry states in his commentary, "Junia could have been a feminine name, and consequently might have been the wife of Andronicus." That they were won for Christ ahead of Paul suggests they may have been converted when Peter preached on the Day of Pentecost. During that feast eight thousand people were accepted into the family of God, and Andronicus and his wife could have been among that number.

A Pardon Accepted . . . *"In Christ"*

It is evident that these people were won for Christ early in the history of the church. The apostle Paul, who then was known as Saul of Tarsus, was later converted outside of the gate of Damascus where he had gone to apprehend Christians. Luke described that event in what is now known as the ninth chapter of the Acts. Paul's sister was a devout Jewess who probably provided a home in which her student brother stayed. It has been assumed that since Saul was never mentioned in the Gospels, he had graduated and returned to Tarsus. Later he came back to Jerusalem to receive a commission from the high priest to search for, and arrest, Christians who had fled to Damascus.

It can only be imagined how this grieved his sister. When the usual routine of the festival was rudely interrupted by the followers of Jesus, the city was in an uproar. The disciples were fearlessly preaching in the streets, and huge congregations were enthralled by their powerful messages concerning the resurrection of Jesus. A tremendous impact was being made on the minds of great crowds, and the news of the healing of the beggar at the gate of the temple increased the excitement. The situation was completely out of control, and the rulers of the city were unable to end the disturbance.

Perhaps that was when Andronicus and Junia first heard the Good News of salvation through Jesus Christ. Their souls were stirred, and as Paul said, "They were in Christ before me." The grace of God did in a moment what the law was unable to do in a lifetime. When a person intelligently believed Christ was the only Savior, that convert immediately became a member of the family of God. The sacrifices and ministry of the priests were no longer required, for Christ was able to

178

supply the needs of all who trusted Him. This teaching contradicted everything taught in Israel, and the anger of the rabbis was quickly aroused. It was widely reported that many of the priests had embraced the new ideas, and for a while it appeared Judaism had received a deathblow. Andronicus and Junia evidently became prominent in the new movement, for Paul indicated in his letter that the activities of this couple attracted the attention of the apostles. It is not known how this was accomplished, but it might have been through their courageous testimony or spontaneous giving to help believers in need. The apostle wrote: "They were of note among the apostles." There were at least eight thousand new converts, but these special people were "not lost in the crowd"—they were outstanding.

A Prayer Answered . . . *"In Christ BEFORE ME"*

And Saul, yet breathing out threatenings and slaughter against the disciples of the Lord, went unto the high priest. And desired of him letters to Damascus to the synagogues, that if he found any of this way, whether they were men or women, he might bring them bound unto Jerusalem (Acts 9:1–2).

When a Christian is in the midst of a storm, it is difficult to believe every cloud has a silver lining. It is hard to be joyful when prayers remain unanswered, and God seems to ignore the grief of His children. The thrills of Pentecost had become memories, for fierce persecution was threatening the lives of the disciples. Stephen, a brilliant young believer, was being stoned to death, and watching every movement was another man at whose feet the clothing of the martyr had fallen. "And Saul was consenting unto his death" (see Acts 8:1). That was only an insignificant shower compared with the hurricane which followed. Luke described the horrors of those days when he wrote: "And at that time, there was a great persecution against the church which was at Jerusalem; and they were all scattered abroad throughout the region of Judaea and Samaria, except the apostles."

What appeared to be a fatal blow to the church proved to

be one of God's greatest blessings. The fierce persecution transformed ordinary believers into itinerant evangelists. The people who were compelled to leave homes and friends went everywhere preaching the Gospel. Somewhere in the area were Paul's kinsmen who fervently loved the Lord. It would be informative to learn what they thought and said when they discovered their relative was responsible for their suffering. Were they ashamed and filled with resentment?

It is written that "Saul made *havock* of the church, entering into every house, and haling men and women committed them to prison" (Acts 8:3). The word translated *havock* is *elumaineto*; it suggests a wild pig using its snout to uproot young plants in a vineyard. *The Englishmen's Greek Testament* translates the verse: "But Saul was ravaging the assembly, house by house entering, and *dragging men and women*, delivered them up to prison." The Christians were pulled through the streets to be thrown into dungeons. That terrible predicament was vastly different from the ecstatic scenes witnessed on the Day of Pentecost. Saul resembled a wild boar uprooting God's garden and had become an instrument of brutality and murder. The terrible situation caused grief to Saul's family who wondered what could prevent further infamy. They prayed, and their intercession played an important part in the miracle which followed. The persecutor became a preacher of the message he had tried to destroy. Every Christian should learn from this account that it pays to pray.

A Passion Acknowledged ... *"Who are of note among the apostles"*

Solomon said: "A good name is rather to be chosen than great riches, and loving favour rather than silver and gold" (Prov. 22:1). It is not known when the king of Israel wrote these words, but his experiences verified the accuracy of his statement. He possessed wealth and wisdom, but his conduct tarnished his reputation. Blessed is the man who stays close to God, for he "shall abide under the shadow of the Almighty" (see Ps. 91:1).

Every pastor knows the members who are worthy of trust

within his church. The people known to Narcissus were *"in the Lord."* Tryphona and Tryphene *"Laboured in the Lord."* The beloved Persis *"Laboured much in the Lord."* This is true of every assembly. The majority of church people claim to be Christians, but they seldom do anything for the Savior. They attend services infrequently, place a gift on the offering plate, and take a week's leave of absence after every Sunday morning service. They never manifest interest in the continuing work of evangelism, but if their faith were challenged, they would be annoyed.

There are other people in the assembly who have a genuine concern for the work of Christ, but they dislike responsibility, for they have many irons in their fire! They enjoy bowling a few nights a week, serve on several committees, and are busy in many areas of activity. These people are willing to assist in any church related program if the effort will not be too time consuming and can be fitted into the regular routine of the week. They are willing to help, but please do not ask too often! It will be difficult to add to the weekly schedule.

Finally, there may be found in every church, members who are the life of the place. They do what is necessary and never complain nor make excuses. These people obey the text which says: "Whatsoever thy hand findeth to do, *do it with thy might*, for there is no work, nor device, nor knowledge, nor wisdom, in the grave whither thou goest" (Eccl. 9:10). Often these faithful souls are the first to arrive in church and the last to leave. They dislike publicity, but if anything worthwhile is going on, somewhere in the background these saints will be working hard to make the project a success. They belong to "The Beloved Persis Committee," and are devoted helpers of all who need assistance. Such people are easily recognized in a small group but difficult to find in a large crowd. Yet in the early church where for a time at least there were eight thousand members, Andronicus and Junia were prominent, and even the twelve apostles were aware of their service for Christ. It would have been enlightening if either Luke or Paul had supplied additional details about these wonderful workers. The fact that they were not "needles hidden in a haystack" says much for their faithfulness which was recognized throughout the city.

A Partnership Appreciated ... *"My fellow prisoners"*

Someone has said: "The man worthwhile is the man who can smile when everything goes dead wrong." There are occasions when "fair weather Christians" lose their fervor in storms! Andronicus and Junia had committed themselves to the Lord, and their devotion prevailed when persecution destroyed their liberty. There was a time during the ministry of the Lord when some of His listeners did not like what He said, and made that an excuse for deserting Him (John 6:66). Others, although they did not understand His message, refused to leave.

It is not known whether Andronicus and Junia were imprisoned with Paul, or if they had been incarcerated in another place, and so were called "fellow prisoners." The great missionary had been arrested on several occasions. Writing to the Corinthians he said he had been "in prison more frequent" (see 2 Cor. 11:23). Accused people were sometimes given the opportunity to recant, but true Christians rejected the opportunity, preferring to suffer with Christ than to enjoy "the pleasures of sin for a season" (see Heb. 11:25). Paul appreciated the courage of his kinsmen and expressed admiration when he wrote his letter to the Romans.

We should never forget the debt owed to the early Christians whose blood became the seed of the church. They left behind an example that all believers should emulate. Without the influence of those pioneers, we would be without the church, the Bible, and hope for eternity. The people of a bygone age gave us a treasure that must never be lost. It was because of their unending dedication we now sing:

> My hope is built on nothing less
> Than Jesus' blood and righteousness;
> I dare not trust the sweetest frame,
> But wholly lean on Jesus's name.
> On Christ, the solid Rock I stand;
> All other ground is sinking sand.

*And lest I should be exalted above measure through the
abundance of the revelations, there was given to me a thorn
in the flesh, the messenger of Satan to buffet me, lest I should
be exalted above measure. For this thing I besought the Lord
thrice, that it might depart from me. And he said unto me, My
grace is sufficient for thee: for my strength is made perfect in
weakness. Most gladly therefore will I rather glory in my
infirmities, that the power of Christ may rest upon me
(2 Cor. 12:7–9).*

A thorn in the flesh is always an annoyance, a painful
intrusion into what might be a perfectly healthy body. The
strange mystical experience endured by Paul bequeathed to
posterity something to be perpetually discussed. His repeated
request for deliverance was denied three times, but the troubled preacher was assured by the Lord, "My grace is sufficient for thee."

A Prevented Description . . . *Fortunate*

And I knew such a man, (whether in the body, or out of the
body, I cannot tell: God knoweth;) How that he was caught
up into paradise, and heard unspeakable words, which it is not
lawful for a man to utter (2 Cor. 12:3–4).

At some point in his life Paul had been given a special
revelation, in which his spirit had been transported to the
third heaven. It is necessary to understand that the Bible speaks
of three heavens: (1) The atmospheric heaven from which
earth receives its weather patterns; (2) The celestial heavens
into which man is now sending exploratory rockets; and (3)
The third heaven which is far out in space, and is the home of
God. Christ ascended into that country and promised to return. Paul was allowed to view scenes and hear words which
he was not permitted to describe nor repeat. It would be foolish to speculate about the details of the apostle's revelation.
God refused to allow His servant to divulge what had been

seen and heard, and it is extremely unlikely that He would give to others what was denied to Paul. Evidently, the apostle saw some of the wonders of the eternal world and heard things unsuitable for publication on earth. The Lord had reasons for enforcing silence upon His messenger, and perhaps someday these will be explained. Solomon said there was a time to speak, and another to remain silent. Paul would have agreed with that statement (see Eccl. 3:7).

A Probable Danger . . . *Foreseen*

And lest I should be exalted above measure through the abundance of the revelations (2 Cor. 12:7).

God gave to the church an example of His care for the work of His servants. When Moses died, the Lord became an undertaker. It was written: "So Moses the servant of the LORD died there in the land of Moab, according to the word of the LORD. And he buried him in a valley in the land of Moab, over against Beth-peor: but no man knoweth of his sepulchre unto this day" (Deut. 34:5–6).

There was a danger the children of Israel might make that grave into a shrine. Therefore, God refused to disclose where the body of their leader had been interred. Paul may have considered that fact when he urged the early Christians to walk circumspectly. Dr. G. Campbell Morgan illustrated that verse with a cat walking carefully along the top of a garden wall. Surrounded by many pieces of broken glass that had been secured in cement, the animal walked slowly and was never cut. The apostle was already admired by a great company of people, and the Lord was aware that immature converts might think more highly of their leader than of the cause he represented.

Paul was like Elijah, "a man of like passions as we are." Had he been less devoted to his Master, his ego might have been inflated. His words are illuminating. "Lest any man should think of me above that which he seeth me to be, or that he heareth of me" (2 Cor. 12:6). The church in Corinth was already divided into factions where members admired various

184

leaders. Even some of the apostle's supporters might have been tempted to make certain claims to support their arguments if they had known what had been seen and heard in heaven. If the apostle had been permitted to describe what happened in the eternal world, no building nor amphitheater would have been sufficiently large to accommodate the congregation. When men attract more attention to themselves than to the Lord, they cease being *God's* servants.

A Painful Deterrent . . . *Frightening*

There was given to me a thorn in the flesh, the messenger of Satan to buffet me, lest I should be exalted above measure (2 Cor. 12:7).

The apostle never suspected his statement would become part of every language. Any persistent problem is described as "A thorn in the flesh." Numerous ideas have been expressed, but the consensus seems to be that Paul suffered from a chronic eye disease. Some think it was the result of what happened near to the entrance to Damascus, when a light, above the brightness of the noonday sun, shone upon the would-be persecutor. Paul wrote one of his shortest letters to the believers in Galatia, and explained: "Ye see how large a letter I have written unto you with mine own hand" (Gal. 6:11). *The Amplified Bible* translates this verse: "(Mark carefully these closing words of mine.) See with what *LARGE LETTERS* I am writing this with my own hand."

That suggests a person with his face close to the parchment, someone obliged to use large letters to see what had been stated. Most of Paul's letters were written by friends who were trying to assist their beloved leader. If this interpretation is correct, he endured severe hardship as he traveled thousands of miles on his missionary journeys. His inability to read small script explains why he called his affliction "the messenger of Satan." Paul had no time to consider his experiences in heaven, for he was continually struggling against circumstances beyond his control.

Some theologians believe the apostle's thorn in the flesh

was a quick temper; when his anger was aroused he could be very forthright in his denunciation of opponents (see Acts 23:1–5). His problem, whatever it might have been, was continually annoying, and it is not difficult to understand his frustration when a perfectly legitimate request was refused by the Lord.

A Personal Desire . . . *Frustrated*

There was given to me a thorn in the flesh, the messenger of Satan to buffet me, lest I should be exalted above measure. For this thing I besought the Lord thrice, that it might depart from me. And he said unto me, My grace is sufficient for thee: for my strength is made perfect in weakness (2 Cor. 12:7–9).

Paul was a great man of prayer, but since he asked the Lord to help him on three different occasions, it may be assumed he was desperate. It is significant that he never asked the fourth time. Elijah sent his servant up the mountain seven times before he was convinced help was about to arrive (see 1 Kings 18:43). To the everlasting credit of Paul, it should be said when the Lord told him, "My grace is sufficient for thee," the apostle never repeated his prayer. He recognized that God's grace was more to be desired than alleviation from personal discomfort. Someone has used an acrostic to explain the grace of God: "*G*reat *R*iches *A*t *C*hrist's *E*xpense." Webster's Dictionary defines grace as "The free unmerited love and favor of God." This statement corresponds with another made by the apostle. "There hath no temptation taken you but such as is common to man: but God is faithful, who will not suffer you to be tempted above that ye are able; but will with the temptation also make a way to escape, that ye may be able to bear it" (see 1 Cor. 10:13).

God's grace is the antidote for every troublesome circumstance; it is the balm of Gilead to promote peace when disturbances become overwhelming. The writer to the Hebrews wrote, "Let us therefore come boldly unto the throne of grace, that we may obtain mercy, and find grace to help in time of need" (Heb. 4:16). When a man worships in the presence of

186

God and remembers the blessings already received, it is impossible to be critical, complaining, and self-centered. When grace floods the soul, a trusting believer sees not the blackness of the sky, but the brilliance of the stars.

Charles Haddon Spurgeon, the famous British preacher, was returning to his home after a very difficult day in the city of London. He was oppressed and disconsolate when suddenly a text came to his mind. "My grace is sufficient for thee." His laughter became almost uncontrollable as he said, "Of course; of course. God's grace is sufficient for me." All Christians should know that grace is better than gloom. One entrances the soul; the other engulfs the spirit. David asked, "Why art thou cast down, O my soul, and why art thou disquieted within me? Hope thou in God; for I shall yet praise him, who is the health of my countenance, and my God" (Ps. 42:11).

A Present Deliverer . . . *Favored*

Most gladly therefore will I rather glory in my infirmities, that the power of Christ may rest upon me. Therefore I take pleasure in infirmities, in reproaches, in necessities, in persecutions, in distresses for Christ's sake; for when I am weak, then am I strong (2 Cor. 12:9–10).

It should be remembered that Paul was describing "a thorn in the flesh" which had been given to him fourteen years earlier. He realized how God's grace had been sufficient for all his need. The promised help had transformed his life and turned difficulties into delights, persecution into pleasure, infirmities into inspiration. Perhaps prior to the beginning of his problems, he had relied upon his own ingenuity and self-sufficiency. When these failed, he learned to rest upon the promises of God. His words were impressive—*"That the power of Christ may rest upon me."* He was not referring to a former vision, but to a continuing experience which began when the power of the Holy Spirit came upon him as the mantle of Elijah had fallen upon Elisha.

He wrote: "When I am weak, then am I strong." This understanding made it impossible to boast of anything except the Cross. It is challenging to read his words: "Therefore I take pleasure in infirmities, reproaches, necessities, persecution." Every human instinct would rebel against such inconveniences, but evidently Paul had reached an exalted plateau of spirituality where the casual had been replaced by the extraordinary. The life of Christ was flooding his soul. He no longer looked at his problems, but at the omniscient Lord controlling his life. "That the power of Christ may rest upon me." This was the secret of Paul's success, for his experiences were sometimes strange and exasperating. Comparing himself with critics, he wrote:

Are they ministers of Christ? (I speak as a fool) I am more: in labours more abundant, in stripes above measure, in prisons more frequent, in deaths oft. Of the Jews five times received I forty stripes save one. Thrice was I beaten with rods, once was I stoned, thrice I suffered shipwreck, a night and a day I have been in the deep. In journeyings often, in perils of waters, in perils of robbers, in perils by mine own countrymen, in perils by the heathen, in perils in the city, in perils in the wilderness, in perils in the sea, in perils among false brethren; In weariness and painfulness, in watchings often, in hunger and thirst, in fastings often, in cold and nakedness. Beside those things that are without, that which cometh upon me daily, the care of all the churches (2 Cor. 11:23–28).

It was remarkable that during these crises the power of Christ sustained the apostle. The source of such help is still available. It would be of great help if every Christian worker prayed:

> Cleanse me from my sin, Lord:
> Put Thy power within, Lord,
> Take me as I am, Lord,
> And make me all Thine own.
> Keep me day by day, Lord,
> Underneath Thy sway, Lord:
> Make my heart, Thy palace,
> And Thy royal throne.

This is a faithful saying, and worthy of all acceptation
(1 Tim. 1:15).

The epistles written by Paul to Timothy and Titus were personal, practical, and powerful. The apostle was addressing two of his favorite sons and advising them what to preach to their congregations. Solomon, the king of Israel, did a similar job. He wrote proverbs considered to be pearls of wisdom, but what he said was ruined by deplorable conduct. He gave advice which should have been applied to himself. Paul was completely different. He was a leader of the Christian church, had evangelized the known world, and inscribed the name of Jesus on millions of hearts and minds. At the beginning of his ministry there was only one Christian church. It was situated in the city of Jerusalem. Yet before he went home to heaven, the apostle established churches in every major city in the Roman empire. His fame outshone that of any other disciple, and his inspired letters were destined to be read worldwide.

He understood the problems which would confront young pastors and realized they would make mistakes and become discouraged. Paul had been hurt by Christians who did not exhibit the beauty of the Savior. They tried to undermine his ministry; their criticism was cruel and unrelenting. Yet the apostle never wavered from his duty. The advice offered came from personal experience. His three epistles are called *The Pastoral Epistles*; they should be studied by every minister. Young preachers begin their work with boundless enthusiasm and plan to save the world overnight. They become discouraged when, after years of service, they believe themselves to be failures. The task of discovering new materials can be frustrating, and preparing for regular church services may be boring. A man who studies for long periods of time may be disappointed when friends neglect to say "Thank You." Many devoted ministers go to church filled with expectations but return to their homes wondering if they wasted their time.

As far as is known, Paul did not possess a degree in

psychology, but, inspired by the Holy Spirit, he wrote three textbooks which are now studied in universities. It seems significant that when he considered the tasks ahead of his young protégés, he emphasized certain things. Every word he wrote was wise and necessary, but some details were more vital than others. What Paul was about to express was very important, for without this information his friends might fail in their ministry. He seemed to be saying: "Everything I tell you is important, but *this* is a faithful saying and worthy of all acceptation." Three times to Timothy and once to Titus he seemed to be saying: "Whatever you say in your sermons, *never leave this out.* If you do, you may preach and say nothing."

The Undeserved Grace . . . *Redemption*

This is a faithful saying, and worthy of all acceptation, that Christ Jesus came into the world to save sinners; of whom I am chief (1 Tim. 1:15).

When Paul arrived in the city of Corinth, he was determined to preach about the death of the Savior. An important lesson had been learned on Mars Hill in Athens, where reasoning only produced arguments. When he left, the apostle believed he had failed in his mission. It probably took two days or more to walk to Corinth, and during the journey he had plenty of time to reflect. When later he wrote to the church that he established, he said:

And I, brethren, when I came to you, came not with excellency of speech or of wisdom, declaring unto you the testimony of God. For I determined not to know any thing among you, save Jesus Christ, and him crucified (1 Cor. 2:1–2).

The apostle's phenomenal success in Corinth set the pattern for the rest of his ministry. The Hebrews in whose synagogues he preached detested the Gospel, for it was to them a stumbling block. When Paul used the Old Testament to support his claims, the listeners had no effective reply and were

190

left irritated. The intellectual Greeks despised the Gospel, for they thought redemption through sacrifice was ridiculous. When Jews and Greeks united to oppose the evangelist, progress became extremely difficult. The life of the apostle was threatened and his services interrupted. Yet through all the difficulties he continued to preach about the death of Christ. He remained so convinced about the validity of the message that he expressed extreme disapproval of any other doctrine (see Gal. 1:6–9).

One wonders what Paul would say if he were writing to students in modern seminaries. Men and women are trained to be administrators, counselors, and social workers, but it is doubtful if they are instructed how to knock on doors and explain to strangers the mighty power of the Cross of Christ. Some pastors are more successful in dividing churches than in leading souls to Christ. I attended a banquet in honor of a retiring president of a prestigious Baptist College who said: "If I could have my time over again, I would preach nothing but the old time Gospel of Jesus." I wished that statement had been made at the commencement of his ministry instead of at its end! Paul insisted that Christ came into the world to save sinners, of whom he was the chief. When men preach without mentioning the reconciling death of the Savior, it is evident they are in the wrong occupation.

The apostle said his message was conceived in the mind of God, fulfilled in the death of Jesus, and should be the theme of every message preached. There never was, nor is, nor will be an effective substitute for the Gospel of Christ. If Timothy, Titus, and Paul preached it, so should every clergyman. To try to save the world with any other message is as futile as trying to empty the ocean with a teaspoon.

The Unhindered Growth ... *Rewarding*

For bodily exercise profiteth little: but godliness is profitable unto all things, having promise of the life that now is, and of that which is to come. This is a faithful saying, and worthy of all acceptation (1 Tim. 4:8–9).

During the lifetime of Paul there existed many sects and cults which practiced all kinds of exercises to "keep people in shape." The Olympic Games and other sporting events in Rome and throughout the empire were so popular that thousands of athletes could be seen daily throwing javelins, hurling the discus, and running in marathons to prepare for forthcoming events. Perhaps there were Christians who spent more time with their exercises than with their Lord. There was nothing wrong with programs to develop physical strength, unless they prevented spiritual growth. The apostle realized his friends would be required to offer guidance to men and was careful when supplying advice. He did not condemn the activities, but did say: "They profiteth little." Some activities developed muscles, others decreased weight, but they were all meant to improve appearance and impress friends. Paul compared these with godliness which pleased the Lord.

All Christians are running in the race of life and are hopeful to win a prize. If athletes were willing to sacrifice enticing food, practice endlessly, and refuse to permit interference with their daily routines, such determination should be more necessary for followers of the Savior. God will reward overcomers. Contrasting persevering athletes with inspired saints, Paul reminded his readers that earthly crowns would perish; those given by Christ would endure eternally. Contestants who ruined their chances of victory by eating and drinking would be their own enemies, for sacrifice is the forerunner of success. The believers in Galatia forgot that fact, and the apostle wrote to them, saying: "O foolish Galatians, who hath bewitched you? . . . Are ye so foolish? having begun in the Spirit, are ye now made perfect by the flesh?" (Gal. 3:1–3).

Contestants in the marathon of life should avoid anything which undermines their chances of victory. Paul believed it necessary for Timothy and Titus to emphasize this fact. The birth of a child should cause abounding happiness, but if the baby never learns to walk and talk, joy is replaced by sadness. The apostle explained how he had suffered because of his faith in the Savior of the world. He said to his colleagues: "These things, *command* and teach."

The Unchanging God . . . *Remaining*

It is a faithful saying: For if we be dead with him, we shall also live with him . . . He abideth faithful: he cannot lie (2 Tim. 2:11, 13).

A secure anchor is an asset when a ship is being buffeted by a storm, and an irrefutable fact is reassuring when a soul is overwhelmed by adversity. Paul spoke about suffering, disease, and denial because he realized Timothy would encounter them all during his ministry. There would arise many questions which would be difficult to answer, and problems too hard to solve. Nevertheless, God would be faithful and would never deny access to Himself. When faith is lost, nothing remains. Job realized this when in the midst of his difficulties, he exclaimed: "Though he slay me, yet will I trust in him" (Job 13:15).

Paul mentioned very important conditions, all of which were vital to successful Christian living. (1) "For *if* we be dead with him, we shall also live with him" (2 Tim. 2:11). The apostle explained in his letter to the Romans that spirit-filled believers are identified with Christ in His death, and this was the divine plan for spiritual success. The carnal life—the "old Adam"—would retaliate, argue, be spiteful and unforgiving, but if this nature were nailed to the Cross, believers would experience an outpouring of resurrection power. Timothy was urged to explain this to his congregation.

(2) "*If* we suffer we shall also reign with him" (v. 12). Writing to the Ephesians, Paul said Christians are seated with Christ "in heavenly places, far above principalities, and powers and the rulers of darkness." Provision has already been made whereby saints could trample under foot the lusts to which they were formerly enslaved; but believers were reminded this had to be personally appropriated.

(3) "*If* we deny him, he also will deny us" (v. 12). This statement had broad implications. Cooperation was necessary to bring blessing to believers. If they refrained from doing the will of God, the Lord could not bless them. Jesus promised that all things would be added to the disciples *if* they sought

193

first the kingdom of God (see Matt. 6:33). Unless that condition were met, no person could receive God's benediction.

(4) *"If* we believe not, yet he abideth faithful: he cannot deny himself"* (v. 13). Doubts may attack the mind and, if permitted to remain, may destroy faith. Nevertheless, the immutability of the Almighty does not depend upon the changing whims of disappointed people. God will always be what He was. He is "the same yesterday, and today, and for ever" (see Heb. 13:8). A cloudy day does not mean the sun has ceased to exist. May Agnew Stephens was correct when she wrote:

> Have faith in God; the sun will shine;
> Though dark the clouds may be today;
> His heart hath planned your path and mine,
> Have faith in God; have faith alway.

The Unique Goal . . . *Responsibility*

> This is a faithful saying, and these things I will that thou affirm constantly, that they which have believed in God might be careful to maintain good works (Titus 3:8).

It has been conjectured that Titus, Paul's associate, was older than Timothy and more diplomatic. He arbitrated in some of the problems which troubled the church at Corinth. He was a Gentile (Gal. 2:3) who became the first bishop of Crete. He must have been cautious, wise, and understanding, for intervening in church quarrels was never an easy matter. Paul trusted him implicitly.

It would appear from this letter that the apostle did not repeat all that was written to Timothy. Yet there was always need for holiness in the lives of Christians wherever they lived or worked. Titus was an arbitrator in Corinth, a fellow laborer with Paul in Jerusalem, an itinerant preacher on missionary journeys, and a bishop over the diocese of Crete. He reached all types of people, in all kinds of places, and ministered to all ages in all circumstances. His message was essential to every one of his listeners, for they were living epistles, seen and read of all men. He wrote: "These things I will that thou affirm constantly." "Titus, my brother, when you preach, say something!"

These thoughts were uppermost in the mind of Paul when he wrote this letter to his young friend. Christians should be careful what they present by life and lip, for people watch more intently than they listen. One moment of self-indulgence may ruin a lifetime of preaching. John would have endorsed Paul's message, for he wrote: "He that saith he abideth in Christ ought himself so to walk, even as he walked" (1 John 2:6). Someone has skillfully handled the letters in the word Christian, Christ-I-A-N. If the last three letters are omitted (I-I; A-am; N-nothing), only Christ remains, and that must always be the standard for holy living and successful service.

For I am now ready to be offered, and the time of my departure is at hand. I have fought a good fight, I have finished my course, I have kept the faith (2 Tim. 4:6–7).

The final words spoken by anyone are seldom forgotten. They are important, for they express the last thoughts of a person about to leave this world. For example, during my stay in Canada, my mother went to be with the Lord. I had been away a long time and had tried to persuade her to join me. She was scared of airplanes, but finally agreed to come. Unfortunately, sickness spoiled her plans. She wrote a letter explaining she had to undergo surgery, but promised to come immediately after her hospital stay terminated. She wrote: "If the plane goes down, I shall be with your dad; if it does not, I shall be with you, but in any case I *shall meet you in the morning!*"

The same truth applied to Paul, the brave missionary who evangelized the world and introduced innumerable people to the Savior. It would have been nice had he written an autobiography, for the book would have enthralled millions of readers. However, his motto seemed to have been "*not I but Christ.*" He expressed a lifetime in three majestic verses, and a simple epitaph will reflect excellence throughout eternity. It supplied six word pictures of exceptional beauty.

A Sacrifice . . . *Prepared*

For I am now ready to be offered.

It is interesting that Paul said, "I am ready to be offered." He was ready to lay down his life for the Lord he adored. He did not say he was ready to die! He used different terminology—he was ready and willing to be sacrificed, to make his final commitment. The sacrifices offered in the temple were without blemish. They were completely for Jehovah, and never returned to service. Evidently Paul had reached such a place in his own life, and he was eagerly anticipating entering into the presence of his Savior. The apostle realized he was about to become a martyr, but thoughts of an imminent decease never disturbed the tranquillity of his soul; his vision was focused on meeting Christ.

Paul had been present when the first martyr went home to heaven and had not forgotten that experience. He heard Stephen saying: "Behold, I see the heavens opened, and the Son of man standing on the right hand of God" (see Acts 7:56). The apostle could not forget how he had become a recipient of God's grace. The young Christian had prayed for his murderers, saying, "Lord lay not this sin to their charge." All through life he had remembered that prayer and finally felt worthy to follow Stephen into the presence of Christ. He was to become a sacrifice of praise.

A Sailor . . . *Preparing*

The time of my departure is at hand.

Paul knew his sojourn on earth was ending; his ship was soon to sail for another country! The Greek word translated "departure" is *analuseo*, which suggests two things. The verb *luseo* means to loose or liberate, to set free. The prefix *ana* suggests the beginning of a journey. To use the language of a seaman, his anchor was being raised; his voyage would soon begin. Earlier in his ministry Paul indicated to the Philippians that he had a desire to go immediately to heaven but realized it was necessary to strengthen the church and bring them closer to Christ (see Phil. 1:23–24). That desire had been fulfilled, and there remained no valid reason why his departure should be delayed. He had already claimed to be a citizen of heaven, and he joyfully anticipated his homegoing (see Phil. 3:20). He had no luggage, for the journey would soon be completed. One moment he would be absent from the body and the next, present with the Lord! All that was needed for eternity awaited his arrival.

> Earth had lost its great attraction;
> Heaven alone could satisfy:

He was going home to Heaven
Where he knew he'd never die.

A Soldier . . . *Persevering*

I have fought a good fight.

Paul's life had been difficult; he had enlisted in God's army and had never run from danger. Many of the early followers of the Savior had left their Leader, and even a few of his own associates had gone away. He wrote: "Only Luke is with me" (see 2 Tim. 4:11). The apostle had continued his conflict, and although the scars of battle remained, he was about to receive a commendation from his Commander-in-Chief.

The apostle mentioned three enemies: the world, the flesh, and the devil. Christians are sometimes awed by the magnitude of Paul's achievements and forget that he was like other people. When he wrote to the Christians in Rome, he said, "For I know that in me, (that is, in my flesh,) dwelleth no good thing: for to will is present with me; but how to perform that which is good I find not. For the good that I would I do not; but the evil which I would not, that I do" (Rom. 7:18–19). There were occasions when unholy thoughts entered his mind, but when this happened, the apostle leaned heavily upon the everlasting arms of God's kindness. The enemy was relentless, but Paul triumphed because he resisted the wiles of the devil. It was remarkable that at the end of his career, this brave warrior for Christ could say: "I have fought a good fight."

A Sportsman . . . *Prevailing*

I have finished my course.

When this great leader spoke of finishing his course, he might have been thinking about the Olympic Games for which many athletes prepared throughout their lifetime. The writer to the Hebrews compared the Christian life with the experiences of Jesus. He wrote: "Let us run with patience the race that is set before us, looking unto Jesus the author and finisher of our faith; who for the joy that was set before him endured the cross, despising the shame, and is set down on the right hand of the throne of God" (Heb. 12:1–2). The Savior had also been running a difficult race, but had triumphed gloriously. He never became a dropout. Probably the light of heaven was already shining upon Paul's face when he wrote: "I have finished my course." He had reached the winning post, and was already approaching the royal throne where the King of Kings was waiting to offer His congratulations.

As Paul reminisced, he remembered when adversity almost overwhelmed his spirit, and he had been beaten to his knees. He summed up his experiences by saying: "In labours more abundant, in stripes above measure, in prisons more frequent, in deaths oft, of the Jews five times received I forty stripes save one. Thrice was I beaten with rods, once was I stoned, thrice I suffered shipwreck, a night and a day have I been in the deep: In journeyings often, in perils of waters, in perils of robbers, in perils by mine own countrymen, in perils by the heathen, in perils in the city, in perils in the wilderness, in perils in the sea, in perils among false brethren; in weariness and painfulness; in watchings often, in hunger and thirst, in fastings often, in cold and nakedness. Beside those things that are without, that which cometh upon me daily, the care of all the churches" (2 Cor. 11:23–28). Had the apostle been asked to explain his success, he would have replied: "I can do all things through Christ which strengtheneth me" (see Phil. 4:13).

A Security Guard . . . *Protecting*

I have kept the faith.

The apostle had been entrusted with a jewel of incalculable worth. The Gospel of God's redeeming grace had to be guarded carefully. Jewish teachers and Gentile unbelievers would sacrifice everything they possessed to destroy the good news of salvation. Their efforts had to be resisted constantly. Some important officials had said Paul was mentally unbalanced, and his message was false. Yet through everything, he remained true to his commission; he never changed. The message had been a stumbling block to the Jews, and foolishness to the Greeks. He had been an object of scorn to many of the intellectuals of his generation. As Dr. Frederich Schleiermacher, the eminent German theologian, said: "Nothing changes the fact that Paul's theology was that of a converted man." Evidently, he believed if Christ could transform a persecutor into a preacher, there was no man beyond the reach of the grace of God. The apostle was so convinced his Gospel was the only Gospel, he issued the greatest denunciation of all other doctrines. In this modern age, Paul would have been an unpopular evangelist. Writing to the Galatians he said: "But though we, or an angel from heaven, preach any other gospel unto you than that which we have preached unto you, let him be accursed" (Gal. 1:8). Paul would have appreciated the words of Sir John Bowring:

> In the cross of Christ I glory,
> Tow'ring o'er the wrecks of time;
> All the light of sacred story
> Gathers round its head sublime.
>
> Bane and blessing, pain and pleasure,
> By the cross are sanctified;
> Peace is there that knows no measure,
> Joys that through all time abide.

A Sovereign's Delight . . . *Proclaimed*

Henceforth there is laid up for me a crown of righteousness, which the Lord, the righteous judge, shall give me at that day: and not to me only, but unto all them also that love his appearing (2 Tim. 4:8).

Paul knew what it meant to stand before councils, magistrates, kings and queens. Unafraid, he had been questioned by skilled attorneys and had been paraded before people of great eminence. Now he was confronted by his greatest experience. When Governor Wallace of Alabama was asked by a news

200

reporter what had been the outstanding moment of his life, he replied: "It has not yet come. The greatest time in my life will come when I meet my Savior face to face." Paul would have applauded that answer.

Maybe he tried to visualize the time when he would again meet the Prince of Peace. The writer to the Hebrews, after mentioning many Old Testament characters, said: "Seeing we are encompassed about with so great a cloud of witnesses . . . " The Living Bible supplies an interesting translation of that text. "Since we have such a huge crowd of men of faith *watching us from the grandstands.*" Perhaps Paul anticipated the moment when multitudes of angels and redeemed saints would cheer as he approached God's throne to receive his reward. His soul would be elated as the Lord offered His congratulations and placed a crown of righteousness upon his head. He would have appreciated the old hymn:

> When all my labors and trials are o'er,
> And I am safe on that beautiful shore,
> Just to be near the dear Lord I adore,
> Will through the ages be glory for me.
>
> Oh, that will be glory for me, glory for me.
> When by His grace I shall look on His face,
> That will be glory, be glory for me.

> *Wherefore seeing we also are compassed about with so great*
> *a cloud of witnesses, let us lay aside every weight, and the sin*
> *which doth so easily beset us, and let us run with patience the*
> *race that is set before us. Looking unto Jesus, the author and*
> *finisher of our faith; who for the joy that was set before him*
> *endured the cross, despising the shame, and is set down at the*
> *right hand of the throne of God (Heb. 12:1–2).*

"The Olympic Games were the most popular of the four festivals held in ancient Greece. They began hundreds of years before Christ, and were held every four years at Olympia. At first, the contests were reserved exclusively for athletes of that country, and from their inauspicious beginning, the games increased in importance until they attracted international attention. As time progressed new items were added to the original program, and the last race was for men clad in suits of armor. These runners were asked to complete two lengths of the stadium. Olympia was not a city, but a religious center where many of the statues of Grecian gods had been installed.

Funk and Wagnall's Encyclopedia tells us that athletes who lived in foreign countries were encouraged to bring their offerings to the gods, and display their prowess in the competitions which followed. According to the accepted belief, the earliest, and for long, the only contest was the *stadion*, or short foot race run over a distance of 630 feet. In the year 724 B.C. the *diaulos*, a race covering two lengths of the stadium, was introduced and four years later the *dolichos*, a long race of about 15,120 feet was arranged, when the contestants discarded the loincloth and ran naked. This custom was followed for many years. As time progressed wrestling, horse racing, chariot racing and other contests were added. The celebrations were held every four years until 194 A.D. when they were suppressed by the Roman Emperor, Theodosius, on the grounds they violated the spirit of Christianity. The first modern Olympic Games were held in April, 1896, and attracted athletes from the United States, Great Britain, and eleven other countries."

The popularity of the ancient contests was evident when other nations began to emulate the example set by Greece. I have sat in the amphitheaters of ancient Ephesus, Petra, and the Colosseum in Rome. The gladiatorial combats where men fought to the death were some of the most repulsive scenes of ancient history. Excitement over these contests was very prevalent when the New Testament was being written, and it was to be expected that reference would be made to these attractions. The verses quoted at the beginning of this study are an example of that possibility. *The Living Bible* translates the text as follows:

Since we have such a huge crowd of men of faith watching us from the grandstands, let us strip off anything that slows us down, or holds us back, and especially those sins that wrap themselves so tightly around our feet, and trip us up; and let us run with patience the particular race that God has set before us (Heb. 12:1 TLB).

Mention has already been made of the discarding of the loincloth worn by ancient athletes. Probably during a contest the garment became loose, and sliding down the legs of the runner, entangled his feet, causing a serious loss of time. The writer to the Hebrews used this illustration to warn Christians against such danger. The entire scenario presented in the twelfth chapter of Hebrews suggests scenes from the Olympic Festivals.

The Watching Audience... *Hopeful*

We are encompassed about with so great a cloud of witnesses—
(men of faith, watching from the grandstands.)

The eleventh chapter of Hebrews has been called "God's Hall of Fame." It is a great title, for the record supplies a list of famous people. From Abel to Abraham and Isaac to Moses and David, readers are introduced to many of God's prominent servants of whom the Almighty was proud. "They were stoned, they were sawn asunder, were tempted, were slain with the sword: they wandered in sheepskins and goatskins; being destitute, afflicted, tormented; . . . they wandered in deserts and in mountains, and in dens and caves of the earth" (Heb. 11:37–38). Deprived of all material comforts, they were pilgrims filled by faith. "And these all, having obtained a good report through faith, received not the promise: God having provided some better thing for us, that they without us should not be made perfect" (Heb. 11:39–40). The text suggests the ancient spiritual athletes had finished their course and were watching our progress from the grandstands of eternity. Does this mean that loved ones who have preceded us into the presence of God are able to watch as we complete our journey? Will they applaud as we cross the finishing line and are welcomed into the presence of Christ?

The Weakening Athlete . . . *Hindered*

Let us lay aside every weight. Let us strip off everything that slows us down . . . especially those sins that wrap themselves so tightly around our feet and trip us up.

It is a cause for regret when an athlete who has consistently led the contestants begins to lose ground. Sometimes this can be prevented. To remember again the incident when the loincloth was discarded, failure may be prevented by resolution. No runner can give an excellent performance if he carries excessive weight. It was a simple matter to shed a loincloth, although the action caused embarrassment. The writer to the Hebrews did not suggest that believers should remove their clothing. The Christian race had nothing to do with garments. This advice referred to habits, customs, and anything capable of impeding spiritual progress. Sometimes affairs of the heart entangle feet. Any man who straps a load of cement to his back prior to a race advertises his stupidity.

The early Christians were urged to examine their equipment and discard anything unnecessary for the approaching challenge. It was interesting that the author differentiated between weights and sin which easily beset the runners. Even legitimate desires may be hindrances. Dedicated believers should never ask, "Is it wrong?" It is wiser to ask, "Is it necessary?" There is never need to analyze evil. Arguments cannot transform sin into righteousness. Athletes, whether they are running the race of life or competing in an international contest, must be ardent in training, anxious to win, and relentless in preparing for the events. Weakening runners never arouse cheers which are only earned by courage; disappointment always follows dropouts.

The Wise Advice... *Helpful*

Let us run with patience the race that is set before us, Looking unto Jesus the author and finisher of our faith.

There are three kinds of contestants: (1) The man who starts well but soon tires. He never makes any special effort, nor displays enthusiasm. Ultimately, he drops back and becomes an "also ran." When Paul wrote to the Galatians, he asked an important question: "Ye did run well; who did hinder you that ye should not obey the truth?" (Gal. 5:7). As converts they had exhibited great interest, but apathy decreased their speed and ruined any possibility of their becoming victors. (2) Some contestants never intend to win but hope onlookers will know they tried. Such men are never disappointed nor ashamed; they run for the exercise! There are many runners whose heart never inspires their feet. They never hurry, but always succeed in getting nowhere! (3) There are athletes who only think of winning. They look toward the winning post and by every means possible endeavor to be the first runner to reach it. The men who competed in the Roman games did so for the dubious honor of wearing a crown of laurel leaves. Christians hope to win a crown of life which endures eternally.

Almost every athlete has a prototype whose example he tries to emulate. Even small children are attracted to famous sportsmen and throughout their lifetime hope to be like their idol. The same principle applies to Christians. They admire the Savior and acquire an intense yearning to be like Him. The writer to the Hebrews expressed that idea. He urged his

readers to *"look unto Jesus,"* the Divine Athlete who presented the world the most spectacular display of courage ever
seen. To discard every hindrance is not sufficient to win a
race. Runners need inspiration to avoid quitting; they need a
renewal of energy to enable their continuance. Even the Lord
encountered fatigue and weariness when Satan attempted to
thwart His purpose. Yet, "He endured the cross, despising the
shame," and having conquered, "is set down at the right hand
of the throne of God" (Heb. 12:2). When believers follow His
example, they become winners in God's Olympic Games.

The Waiting Acclamation . . . *Happiness*
And is set down at the right hand of the throne of God.

I saw a huge crowd assembling in the main street of
Melbourne, Australia, and wondered what had caused the
excitement. When I asked what was taking place, a man replied,
"Sir, in about five minutes, what is left of the First Australian
division sent to Korea will be coming up this street to place a
wreath on the cenotaph in memory of their fallen comrades.
They were ambushed by the enemy and almost all were killed.
Only a handful survived, and their ship docked last night. We
are here to give them a great welcome." Soon I heard the
music of an approaching band and saw policemen on
motorcycles slowly forcing onlookers to the sidewalks. The
mounted police followed, and afterward the musicians playing
a lively march. Finally, as the small number of soldiers
marched proudly along the street, millions of tiny pieces of
paper came fluttering down from the high buildings.

Excited girls ducked beneath the outstretched arms of the
police, ran into the street to kiss, hug, and embrace the soldiers,
who, in spite of everything, never lost a stride. Seemingly
unperturbed, they maintained their composure and proceeded
on their way. I remember that when I entered Australia, I was
involved in an argument with an unpleasant customs official.
My "welcome" to the country was nothing like that of the
soldiers. The commencement of my stay in the country left
much to be desired.

Some day, at the end of life's journey, I shall reach my true homeland. Will the angels line the streets of gold to cheer? Will the city of God reecho with jubilation when I arrive? Will I be escorted to the throne of God to hear: "Well done thou good and faithful servant . . . enter thou into the joy of thy Lord?" The apostle Peter was contemplating such a moment when he wrote: "If ye do these things, ye shall never fall. For so an entrance shall be ministered unto you abundantly into the everlasting kingdom of our Lord and Savior Jesus Christ" (2 Peter 1:10–11). It should be emphasized that many may not be joyfully received. Peter said: "*If ye do these things.*" Everything will depend upon the quality of service we render on earth.

The elder unto the elect lady and her children (2 John 1).

The second epistle of John should attract the attention of every Christian woman; it is the only book in the Bible addressed to a female. Throughout the history of the church the identity of this recipient has been debated by theologians, and two interpretations have been offered. First, it has been suggested that the apostle was writing to a church and its converts and that the author avoided mentioning names in order to protect his friends from persecution. Secondly, most commentators agree the contents of the letter support the conclusion that John was addressing a specific woman who also had a sister (see verse 13). A home is mentioned into which false teachers were not to be granted admittance. It might be claimed the letter would apply in both situations.

The fact that the addressee remained unidentified might have been inspired, for the letter may now be considered a message to every Christian mother. Perhaps this woman had not gained a place of eminence within the assembly, yet she was one of God's elect. She was Mrs. Somebody who had found favor with God and was sufficiently important that the last surviving apostle considered her to be his friend. Every Christian woman should be able to read the letter and find a message applicable to herself. Today the elect lady and her children could be living anywhere. This brief letter may be considered under four headings.

Be Congratulated . . . *You Are Chosen*

The elder unto the elect lady and her children, whom I love in the truth; and not I only, but also all they that have known the truth. For the truth's sake, that dwelleth in us, and shall be with us for ever. Grace be with you, mercy, and peace from God the Father, and from the Lord Jesus Christ, the Son of the Father, in truth and love (2 John 1–3).

When John wrote this letter, he warned his friend about the

dangers of false teachers. He knew that heresy had challenged the Gospel, and within four brief verses he mentioned *the truth* five times. What was meant by this definition is uncertain. The Savior had said: "I am the way, *the truth*, and the life" (John 14:6). The Lord was the embodiment of all truth, and therefore His statements were accurate and reliable. Was the apostle implying that because the new faith had made her a sister in Christ, the Holy Spirit of truth resided within her soul? John believed what he had heard from Christ, and was concerned that legalism would damage the spiritual health of his friend. Discussing the identity of "the elect lady," Adam Clark says: "I am satisfied the letter was sent to some eminent Christian matron who lived not far from Ephesus, and who was probably a deaconess of the church. It is possible that she had a church in her house where the apostles and traveling evangelists frequently ministered and enjoyed her hospitality. She was well known in the church where many had witnessed or heard of her fidelity, and partaken of her hospitality."[1]

Webster's Dictionary defines election as "The divine choice by God by which persons are distinguished as objects of mercy, become subjects of grace, sanctified and prepared for eternal life in heaven." John therefore looked upon his friend as a woman who had been selected and purified by God, and made worthy of sharing eternal life in God's kingdom. She was "chosen of God and precious" (1 Peter 2:4).

Be Concerned . . . *You Are Commanded*

I rejoiced greatly that I found of thy children walking in truth, as we have received a commandment from the Father. And now I beseech thee, lady, not as though I wrote a new commandment unto thee, but that which we had from the beginning, that we love one another (2 John 4–5).

John was delighted to know the elect lady had transformed her home into a sanctuary where her family worshiped. Her children had not only heard the gospel from their mother, they had emulated her example. Unfortunately many professed believers did not practice what was preached. Their heads were filled with religious ideas, but their feet walked in the wrong direction. This delightful mother was filled with affection. Her conduct exemplified her faith. She not only believed in Christ, she was like Him. If a woman's home is her castle, the elect lady lived in a cathedral.

It was important that within the limited space of three verses, the apostle mentioned the commandments four times. God not only offered advice to His children; he issued commandments which He expected all Christians to obey. The outstanding characteristic of the new faith was the ability to love. Blind observances were not always indicative of affection. The heathen exhibited obedience to traditional ideas when they placed food before their idols. The Lord not only desired to be loved. He commanded His people to share it with their neighbors, and help to unite all nations in one family. This desire had been expressed from the beginning; it was not a new doctrine conceived in the minds of philosophers. Any person who refrained from helping other humans was unworthy of preferential treatment from the Lord. Unless the love of God is shared with other people the church becomes a shrine for dead dogma. No man has the right to enjoy God's forgiving grace unless he shares it with undeserving people.

Be Careful ... *You Are Cautioned*

Look to yourselves, that we lose not those things which we have wrought, but that we receive a full reward. . . . If there come any unto you, and bring not this doctrine, receive him not into your house, neither bid him God speed. For he that biddeth him God speed is partaker of his evil deeds (2 John 8–11).

John was passionately loyal to the doctrine of Christ (v. 9); other messages were unreliable, unauthorized, and evil. The apostle would not be an advocate for the World Council of Churches. The fourth gospel had already been written and was regarded by the assemblies to be inspired and authentic. John and Paul would have shared a common view. Paul said: "But though we, or an angel from heaven, preach any other

210

gospel unto you than that which we have preached unto you, *let him be accursed*" (Gal. 1:8). It is significant that when he had written this message, immediately he repeated his words to impress his readers with the importance of the message (compare Gal. 1:8 and 9). John stressed the fact that any preacher who denied the basic truths of the gospel was antichrist. The idea of compromise to promote fellowship did not even exist in the minds of the two apostles. False teaching was threatening the stability of the church, and John feared persuasive eloquence would undermine the faith of the elect lady and her children. She was instructed to deny the strangers entry into her home and not even to wish them God speed. Christians should be conversant with the doctrine of Christ, and able to recognize anything which denies the faith. That message may be easily summarized.

Who Was the Christ?

John wrote: "In the beginning was the Word, and the Word was with God, and the Word was God. The same was in the beginning with God" (John 1:1–2). "And the Word was made flesh, and dwelt among us, (and we beheld his glory, the glory as of the only begotten of the Father), full of grace and truth" (John 1:14). Later the same apostle said: "That which was from the beginning, which we have heard, which we have seen with our eyes, which we have looked upon, and our hands have handled, of the Word of life; (For the life was manifested, and we have seen it, and bear witness, and shew unto you that eternal life, which was with the Father, and was manifested unto us)" (1 John 1:1–2). Jesus said to Philip: "Have I been so long time with you, and yet hast thou not known me, Philip? he that hath seen me hath seen the Father; and how sayest thou then, Shew us the Father? Believest thou not that I am in the Father, and the Father in me?" (John 14:9–10).

What Was His Mission?

The Savior said: "For God so loved the world, that he gave his only begotten Son, that whosoever believeth in him should

211

not perish, but have everlasting life" (John 3:16). Accepting this fact, the apostle wrote: "If we walk in the light, as he is in the light, we have fellowship one with another, and the blood of Jesus Christ his Son cleanseth us from all sin" (1 John 1:7). The early Christians taught that salvation was made possible through the redeeming death of the Lord. That was the basic principle of the doctrine of Christ; He came to save sinners.

How Was that Mission Accomplished?

John believed (1) Christ died to save men from *the penalty of sin*; (2) He rose from the dead to save them from *the power of sin*; (3) He will return to earth to save His people from *the presence of sin*. He wrote: "Beloved, now are we the sons of God, and it doth not yet appear what we shall be: but we know that, when he shall appear, we shall be like him: for we shall see him as he is" (1 John 3:2). God had made salvation possible, and any person who denied that fact should be avoided. If Paul and John were preachers in today's world, they would probably be known as agitators threatening the unity of the churches. They would refuse to compromise their faith to promote harmony. The modern church needs men of their caliber, for their "Old Time Gospel" is sadly needed in our degraded world.

Be Comforted . . . *I Am Coming*

Having many things to write unto you, I would not write with paper and ink: but I trust to come unto you, and speak face to face, that our joy may be full. The children of thy elect sister greet thee (2 John 12–13).

When John wrote this letter, he had reached the age when writing letters was not his favorite occupation. He wrote five books; his gospel, the Revelation, and three epistles, but the time had arrived when he preferred to speak with people "face to face." He explained this to the elect lady, and also mentioned that fact when he wrote to "the beloved Gaius" (3 John 13–14). When John spoke, he liked to look into the listener's eyes. Maybe he learned this from his Master who said: "Moreover if thy brother shall trespass against thee, go and tell him his fault between thee and him alone: if he shall hear thee, thou hast gained thy brother" (Matt. 18:15). In spite of his great age the apostle was still able to travel, and one of his greatest delights was to meet people who adored his Lord. To see their glowing faces and feel the warmth of their devotion enriched his soul.

Dr. William Barclay, whose expositions of Scripture are acclaimed by innumerable Christians, made an illuminating comment. "There has been much speculation as to who The Elect Lady might be. We mention only two of the suggestions. (a) It has been suggested that *The Elect Lady* is Mary, the mother of our Lord. She was to be a mother to John and he was to be a son to her (John 19:26–27), and a personal letter from John might well be a letter to her. (b) *Kurios* means *Master*; and *Kuria* as a proper name would mean Mistress. In Latin, *Domina* is the same name and in Aramaic, *Martha*; both meaning *Mistress* or *Lady*. It has, therefore, been suggested that the letter was written to Martha of Bethany.

"It may well be that the address is deliberately unidentifiable. The letter was written at a time when persecution was a real possibility. If it were to fall into the wrong hands there might well be trouble. And it may be that the letter is addressed in such a way that to the insider its destination is quite clear, while to the outsider it would look like a personal letter from one friend to another."[2]

It is widely believed that John's letter might apply to an individual within the assembly, or to the church itself. Which interpretation may be valid is difficult to decide, but one fact remains evident. Christians should walk according to the commands expressed in the doctrine of Christ. They should be living, loving epistles of their Master.

---

1. *The Bethany Parallel Commentary on the New Testament* (Minneapolis: Bethany House Publishers, 1985).

2. William Barclay, *The Letters of John and Jude* (Philadelphia: Westminster Press, 1976).

GAIUS—THE NAME SHARED
BY FOUR GREAT MEN

The elder unto the well beloved Gaius, whom I love in the truth (3 John 1).

Scholars have said the meaning of the name Gaius is "I am joyful," and that suggests a very happy occasion when proud parents named their offspring. This was always an important event among Hebrew people, and unlike modern times, the given name often had great significance. The parents of Gaius must have been ecstatic with happiness when they decided what to call their child. It is also interesting to know four men in the early church shared the same honor. It would appear that other families shared this great experience. There is reason to believe that God—the Heavenly Father—had similar thoughts. Each of the four infants grew to be remarkable adults whose conduct pleased the Almighty. The children became leaders in the Christian church, but each exhibited a special characteristic.

Gaius—The Convert . . . *How Decided*

I thank God that I baptized none of you, but Crispus and Gaius (1 Cor. 1:14).

Paul was disturbed and disappointed. He had been told by "the household of Chloe" that the church in Corinth had been divided by quarrelsome members. The people had lost sight of Christ and were arguing about unimportant things. The members of the assembly were becoming excessively proud of heroes. Some admired Paul, but others boasted of their affection for Simon Peter and other leaders. A few claimed that Christ alone was the Head of the church, while the intellectuals appreciated the eloquence of Apollos. People were arguing about believers' baptism and were proud their favorite hero had performed their own ceremony. Paul was disturbed by this terrible situation and his statement "I thank God I only baptized two of you" surely upset his readers. He was not even pleased with the faction which claimed to be his supporters. They were dishonoring Paul, for he believed in the lordship of Christ, who alone was the inspiration in the sacrament of baptism. Converts were not baptized into Paul, nor Cephas, nor Apollos—they were baptized into Christ. Paul appeared to say: "I thank God I only immersed two of you, and I am sure they would never be embroiled in your foolish disputes." Nevertheless, he had baptized two of the converts, and in all probability that was the commencement of their Christian experience. What Gaius was prior to his conversion was never revealed, but evidently he forsook all and followed Christ. His friend, Crispus, had been the ruler of the synagogue (see Acts 18:8) and was an outstanding convert whose profession stirred the city. The transformation of his family was a remarkable victory for Jesus of Nazareth, and possibly Gaius and Crispus were baptized together. Their decision was not made without thought; the anger of the Jewish population would be directed against people thought to be traitors. Paul did not say he wished he had not immersed his friends. He was pleased he had not participated in the baptism of the other foolish people who were disturbing God's family. Gaius and Crispus were two brilliant stars shining against the darkness of their surroundings. The apostle was proud of them. The Christians in Corinth should be as dedicated as their brethren. When Paul referred to his friend, he said: "Gaius mine host, *and of the whole church*, saluteth you" (see Rom. 16:23). This remarkable man must have been wealthy, but when God touched his heart, He reached his pocket!

Gaius—The Courageous... *How Determined*

And the whole city was filled with confusion: and having caught Gaius, Aristarchus, men of Macedonia, Paul's companions in travel, they rushed with one accord into the theatre (Acts 19:29).

The city of Ephesus was in an uproar, for Demetrius, the silversmith, had become a rabble-rouser. He and his colleagues made the silver shrines used in the worship of the goddess

Diana, but the profits from their business had been diminishing. Paul was interfering in the worship of Diana, and the infuriating preacher had to be stopped immediately. Demetrius had addressed a private meeting of the craftsmen, and his speech had aroused their anger. The mob rushed into the street, and seeing Gaius and Aristarchus who were known to be visiting Christians, rushed them into the amphitheater. The noise of the tumult echoed through the city.

And when the townclerk had appeased the people, he said, Ye men of Ephesus, what man is there that knoweth not how that the city of the Ephesians is a worshiper of the great goddess Diana, and of the image which fell down from Jupiter? Seeing then that these things cannot be spoken against, ye ought to be quiet, and to do nothing rashly. For ye have brought hither these men, which are neither robbers of churches, nor yet blasphemers of your goddess. Wherefore if Demetrius, and the craftsmen which are with him, have a matter against any man, the law is open, and there are deputies: let them implead one another. But if ye enquire any thing concerning other matters, it shall be determined in a lawful assembly. For we are in danger to be called in question for this day's uproar, there being no cause whereby we may give account of this concourse. And when he had thus spoken, he dismissed the assembly (Acts 19:35–41).

The appearance and speech of the city official temporarily eased the situation. Had he not arrived in time, the Christians might have been murdered. Their lives were being threatened, and escape seemed to be impossible. The captives never flinched nor offered to recant. When the tumult ceased, they were reunited with Paul, but their safety was only temporary. The news spread quickly, and all the worshipers of Diana would renew their attacks. Caution might have suggested a vacation to provide time for the storm to pass, but determined men never run from danger. Luke, the writer of this story, said:

And after the uproar was ceased, Paul called unto him the disciples, and embraced them, and departed for to go into Macedonia . . . and there accompanied him into Asia, Sopater of Berea; and of the Thessalonians, Aristarchus and Secundus; and Gaius of Derbe, and Timotheus; and of Asia, Tychicus and Trophimus. These going before tarried for us at Troas (Acts 20:1, 4–5).

The Savior said, "No man, having put his hand to the plough, and looking back, is fit for the kingdom of God" (Luke 9:62). Gaius and his friends who narrowly escaped death, had no intention of being pronounced unfit for the Lord's domain. They had taken up their cross, and would carry it until it was exchanged for a crown. Their confession might have been expressed in the words of a modern hymn—"No turning back; no turning back."

Gaius—The Carrier . . . *How Dependable*

And in those days came prophets from Jerusalem unto Antioch. And there stood up one of them named Agabus, and signified by the spirit that there should be great dearth throughout all the world: which came to pass in the days of Claudius Caesar. Then the disciples, every man according to his ability, determined to send relief unto the brethren which dwelt in Judaea: Which also they did, and sent it to the elders by the hands of Barnabas and Saul (Acts 11:27–30).

When that special offering was given to Barnabas and Paul, it became evident their mission would be dangerous. The news that a large sum of money was being carried to Jerusalem by two unarmed men could not remain a secret. Bandits would be a continuing threat, and therefore the two missionaries needed an escort. Probably that explains why Luke said the missionaries were accompanied by seven reliable men among whom was Gaius of Derbe (see Acts 20:4). The guardians of what many considered to be a small fortune had to be trustworthy, for the love of money had already become a snare to people within the church (see Ananias and Sapphira,

Acts 5:1–10). Even Judas had stolen money that was donated to help the Lord and His disciples. The escort would need to be watchful, for an attack could come at any moment, and sufficiently courageous to defend what had been committed to their care. When the church trusted Gaius of Derbe with the responsibility of being one of those guardians, they conferred upon him the greatest honor he ever received. The fact that Luke explained this man came from Derbe, suggested he was not the Gaius seized by the citizens of Ephesus. Paul traveled extensively and consequently had helpers from numerous places. Most commentators believe the two men had different identities.

Gaius—The Charitable... *How Delightful*

Beloved, thou doest faithfully whatsoever thou doest to the brethren, and to strangers; Which have borne witness of thy charity before the church: whom if thou bring forward on their journey after a godly sort, thou shalt do well: Because that for his name's sake they went forth, taking nothing of the Gentiles (3 John 5–7).

This message written by John provided a word picture of the church where a prominent member called Diotrephes had become a dictator. His domineering attitude had disturbed the assembly, for he had become a self-proclaimed deity who worshiped at his own shrine. When John sent a letter to the church, this arrogant man refused to accept it, and his belligerent attitude compelled other Christians to reject the apostle's advice. John's message was unmistakable. He wrote:

Wherefore, if I come, I will remember his deeds which he doeth, prating against us with malicious words: and not content therewith, neither doth he himself receive the brethren, and forbiddeth them that would, and casteth them out of the church (3 John 10).

The question might be asked how Gaius could remain in such a disappointing church. Perhaps he believed a lighthouse should be in a place where its services were needed. Many years ago I listened to a Welsh preacher speaking about the Lord standing outside the church of Laodicea and saying: "Behold I stand at the door, and knock: if any man hear my voice, and open the door, I will come in to him, and will sup with him, and he with me" (Rev. 3:20). The minister paused for a moment and then said, "If the Lord desires to enter your disappointing church, at least, stay in there with Him."

When itinerant evangelists arrived in his community, Diotrephes refused to welcome them and persuaded the church to follow his example. Some of the people may have secretly disagreed with this policy but refrained from opposing their belligerent leader. Standing alone against this outrageous man, Gaius welcomed the young preachers, provided hospitality, and when they left, supplied financial assistance to meet their immediate needs. Ignoring the repercussions which might follow, Gaius accepted the responsibility of helping his brethren in Christ. It would not be difficult to imagine the reaction of the man who loved to have the preeminence among church members. He would be infuriated by opposition within the church.

Some people might question whether or not this Gaius had a separate identify from others bearing his name. Maybe there were only two men or, to go to extremes, one who possessed all the characteristics of the four disciples mentioned in this study. At least it may be said that when the four records are placed together, the world is supplied with an outline of what God expects from His children. It would be wonderful if all the characteristics of the four could be found in one life. It would be even more desirable if every reader of these words could be that person!

SCRIPTURE TEXT INDEX

221

Books by Ivor Powell

Bible Cameos
Bible Gems
Bible Highways
Bible Names of Christ
Bible Nuggets
Bible Oases
Bible Pinnacles
Bible Promises
Bible Windows
Honey from the Rock
Manna From Heaven
Matthew's Majestic Gospel
Mark's Superb Gospel
Luke's Thrilling Gospel
John's Wonderful Gospel
The Amazing Acts
The Exciting Epistle to the Ephesians
David: His Life and Times
What in the World Will Happen Next?